Brutal Giants & The Village King (A Ferriby Fa

By

Calvin Wade

ACKNOWLEDGEMENTS

The task of thanking people for all their incredible support is always a difficult one for fear of forgetting someone. Having had three previous opportunities to thank important people in my life, I will try to keep this one a little briefer.

Massive thanks go out to the following :-

All mine & Alison's family – especially my wife, Alison, who recognises that there will always be a 'new plan' on the horizon and allows me to run with it, no matter how bizarre it may appear.

My friends – especially Chris Ayres, Shaun & Jo McManus, Nick & Sarah Woodward, Carl & Katie McGovern, Andrew & Alison Elkington, Mark & Natalie Sunderland, Andy Sykes and Des Platt....Oprah Winfrey once said something about lots of people will ride with you in the limo, but you need people to ride the bus with you when the limo breaks down...these people have ridden the bus and then pushed it once it stopped.

The 'Speccies' – especially Alan Oliver, who continues to do great work for 'The Christie'. He is a football fanatic, a fundraiser and a friend.

All involved with North Ferriby United – especially John Rudkin, Julie Martin, John Colley, Christopher Norrie, Chris Holbrough, Trev Cunnington, Dave Yeoman, Dave Farrow, Nick Quantrill, Sam Shepherd and Charlie Mullan (from the Hull Daily Mail). I am not sure many people or football clubs would have welcomed us in so warmly.

Finally, thanks to all the people that help me on Twitter – with a special mention to Jason - @jlc360 for his relentless support.

Saturday 8th November 2014 – A Retrospective Introduction

Almost six months have passed since my first football book, 'Another Saturday & Sweet F.A' concluded with Arsenal winning the 2014 FA Cup Final. If you have read that one, you will know that I met up with Alan Oliver, a Mancunian groundhopper known as 'The Casual Hopper' and we travelled through the fourteen round competition together, often joined by several friends and family, including my Dad, Richard and Alan's daughter, Jordan. The fact that one of those friends, Phil Cooper, who joined us for twelve of the fourteen games, was an Arsenal fan, seemed to make it a fitting finale. The journey was over….or so we thought.

After the Final, Alan and I chatted about what we might do next. At the start of the competition, Alan was hoping to raise £1 000 for 'The Christie', a specialist cancer hospital in Manchester. His mother in law, Pat, had died of cancer and sadly, during last season's journey, Alan's own Mum, Hilda, was also taken by the disease. The fundraising had risen to several thousand pounds, thanks to musical and football events, in conjunction with the FA Cup adventure and Alan didn't want to see the momentum that had been gathered fading away.

The early rounds of the FA Cup, prior to the entry of the big boys in the 3rd Round Proper, had seemed particularly exciting and those who have read the book have often commented that the early stuff was the most captivating to read about. Everyone knows about the Premier League, but everyone does not necessarily know about Stourbridge's War Memorial Athletic Ground or that there is a team called Jarrow Roofing Boldon Community Association Football Club. I suggested to Alan that maybe we could do the FA Trophy one year and after a few weeks deliberation, Alan, in his usual forthright, determined manner, came back with a suggestion, aided by his mate, Nathan Foy, that went one better. How about doing the FA Trophy in 2014-15 and the FA Vase in 2015-16?

From my perspective, there was a snag, a major one at that. The FA website displayed the dates of the fixtures and the 1st Qualifying Round games were due to take place on Saturday 1st November. As a family, we hadn't been abroad for four years, but through the kindness and generosity of Alison's Mum and Dad and their friends, Helen and Mike, we were heading to Calahonda in Southern Spain for a week during the children's October half-term, returning Sunday 2nd November, twenty four hours after the FA Trophy games.

Last season, having been through all 14 Rounds of the FA Cup with Alan, his all or nothing attitude had rubbed off on me. If you missed a replay, that was a fail, if you missed a Round, that was definitely a fail, so would doing every round of the FA Trophy, bar one, really do it for me? After giving it a lot of thought, I decided it probably wouldn't. Alan could do the FA Trophy in its entirety, I would join him at the first match to see him off and from there on in, he was on his own, with a few guest visits from yours truly. By the very fact that you are reading this, you have probably guessed that that plan has gone out of the window.

Why have I changed my mind and decided to journey all over the country once more? There are several reasons I can give you. Firstly, football is a team game, but we have discovered over the last twelve months, that supporting is a team game too. I may not make every round of the FA Trophy, but Alan will and that means 'Team Christie' will. This is not, in any way, shape or form, just about me. Secondly, fate and the footballing Gods are already beginning to play their hand and I have a feeling this adventure is going to be incident packed. Thirdly, I love football, in all its guises and to turn down the opportunity of an adventure isn't me being true to myself.

My Dad has already suggested I should quit whilst I'm ahead,

"We were lucky to go twelve rounds last season without a replay, that won't happen again. Do you really want to be trekking down to Kent on a Tuesday night when you have so much else going on in your life?"

The truthful answer to that question is 'Yes, I probably do.'

I guess what I need to do now is to tell the story of what has happened over the last few weeks that has led me to believe that our journey through the FA Trophy 2014-15 is going to be worth reading about and why it is now going to form the middle part of the "Another Saturday & Sweet FA" trilogy!

Saturday 18th October 2014 – FA Trophy Preliminary Round

Warrington Town v Mossley

Attendance 131

In the whole of the FA Cup season last year, it could certainly be argued we never saw a bad game. Ninety minutes into the FA Trophy and we had already witnessed a real shocker. Football is not just about the ninety minutes on the pitch though, there is always a story that goes with it.

Alan Oliver and I are not old friends, but fourteen months after our first meeting at West Didsbury & Chorlton Football Club, I would consider us to be good friends. I knew once the FA Cup finished, it would not be the end of our friendship. My book on our FA Cup story came out the week after the FA Cup Final and with 50p from each copy going to Alan's charity campaign for 'The Christie', it was only natural that we would chat on the phone on a regular basis. Over the summer, after England's limp performance in the World Cup in Brazil, Alan and I met up a couple of times, once in Wigan, when Alan was on his way to a League of Wales game and once at his house in Failsworth, Manchester. Each time, I was armed with paperback copies of the book to pass on to him. The meeting at Alan's house gave me the opportunity to finally meet Alan's long suffering wife, Jo, who has seen many of her weekend's disrupted by Alan's sporting adventures. She seemed a lovely lady and happy to allow Alan to indulge in his groundhopping experience.

A few weeks prior to the Preliminary Round of the FA Trophy, Alan phoned to say the draw had been made and he had decided the starting point for this year's journey would be Warrington Town against Mossley. Al wanted to pick somewhere that was convenient for me, as well as for him (perhaps trying to tempt me in to committing to doing every round bar the one I'd miss when we were in Spain) and Warrington seemed like the ideal choice.

Warrington Town Football Club has been, in recent years, overshadowed by the town's famous Rugby League counterparts. The football club does have a famous son though. Roger Hunt, who played for Warrington for three years in the late 1950's, went on to play for Liverpool and played for England in the 1966 World Cup Final. Their ground is in the shadows of a large Cantilever bridge over the Manchester Ship Canal, hence the reason the ground is called Cantilever Park (or was, as it is now named after the stadium sponsors, so its current name is 'The HG Driver Recruitment Stadium').

I have been to Cantilever Park before but it is almost twenty years since my last visit. I played for Burscough briefly in the mid-1990's and my best mate from my playing days there, Matthew Helme, subsequently joined Warrington Town. Back in those days, Matt can only be described as a party animal. He was a confident lad with a cheeky smile and had a certain charm with the ladies. As he was from Birkdale, we would often go out on a Saturday night into Southport and party until late at the famous old Southport nightclub, the Kingsway. I would like to say Matthew was a bad influence on me, but I enjoyed partying just as much as he did.

When I joined Burscough, they had Matthew on a contract as they thought he may have a career in the game, but he left when manager Russ Perkins left at the end of the 1994-95 season. Matt had played in a successful Birkdale Juniors side, playing in left midfield in front of another player with a bright future, left back, Dominic Matteo, who went on to play for Liverpool and England. Matt was blessed with a huge amount of natural pace and at one point, in the 1995-96 season, went to Manchester City on a week's loan. He trained with the first team that week and I'll always remember him telling me how amazed he was by Niall Quinn's ability, both in the air and on the ground. Nothing came of his trial at City, so he returned to Warrington Town, where he had gone after a very brief spell at Fleetwood. Back in those days, Fleetwood were a North West Counties team rather than the League One side they are today. I even think in Russ Perkins first year there, they were relegated to the North West Counties Division Two, but they were promoted back up whilst he was still there and obviously they have enjoyed many subsequent promotions since. I didn't get to see Matthew play at Fleetwood, but I left Burscough during the 1995-96 season so went over to see him play at Cantilever Park a couple of times. It is therefore over 18 years since my last visit. Matthew's playing days are long behind him now, as are his days clubbing, as, like me, he is happily married, with two young children.

Warrington, as a town, brings back other memories, some more pleasant than others. On the positive side, Warrington Parr Hall is a great little concert venue and I have been to a number of concerts there, including James, Fish (formerly of Marillion) and a band called ALT that were made up of Irish singer songwriter, Andy White, Liam O'Maonlai from Hothouse Flowers and Tim Finn from Split Enz and Crowded House. All brilliant gigs that I have fond memories of going to.

My interest in music almost led to me being in Warrington on the day of the IRA bombing back in March 1993. When I graduated in 1992, I struggled to find work on any Graduate Trainee Schemes, so started applying for jobs that took my fancy in local papers. I applied for one job in Bolton for an independent record chain, Andy's Records. "Andy's" Head Office was in Bury St.Edmunds, Suffolk, but they were expanding their Empire into the North West with several stores including Preston, Southport, Bolton, Wigan and Warrington. The interview I had was with the brother of the owner, Billy Gray, who had a hairstyle like Jon Bon Jovi, Billy Ray Cyrus and Pat Sharp, but despite that, we seemed to get on very well and he offered me a job in their Southport store. I loved working there, despite the wages being awful. I was classed as a "Graduate Management Trainee" which meant I earned £5 a week more than the other Sales Assistants but had to go to other branches in the North West when they were short staffed, so, after petrol costs I was probably earning less than everyone else.

On Monday 15th March 1993, I arrived in the Southport branch to be told by my boss, a great guy and fanatical Manchester United fan, Rick Blanks, that Warrington branch, a busy branch in Golden Square in the town centre, were two staff down through illness and I needed to go over there to help out for a few days. I had worked there before during the Christmas period so knew some of the staff. Once I started back in Warrington, I enjoyed the change of scenery and would nip over to McDonald's each day for my lunch. I was told originally that I would only be needed until the Thursday, but on the Thursday evening, I had a phone call from Rick, at home, to say the lad they were expecting back was still ill and I was needed on Friday and possibly Saturday too. On the Friday evening, Rick rang me again to say the staff member would definitely be back the following day and to return to Southport as normal.

Shortly after midday, on Saturday, 20th March 1993, two small bombs placed in litter bins by the I.R.A, exploded in the Golden Square Shopping Mall, Bridge Street, killing two boys, Johnathan Ball aged three and Tim Parry aged twelve. I remember hearing the news during my lunch break in Southport and fearing for the safety of the staff I had worked with all week. They all escaped unhurt but one unfortunate staff member was witness to the tragedy. It must have been a traumatic event to be caught up in and whilst I, along with the rest of the nation, mourned the death of two young boys, I was thankful that I had not been back in Warrington that day.

So, on Saturday 18th October 2014, I set off to Cantilever Park with a few memories of Warrington milling around in my head. My wife, Alison, is very tolerant of my football supporting exploits, she is by no means a nagging wife, but when she told me her parents, Barry and Paula, were coming over for the day, I could tell she was disappointed when I said I would not be around as I was heading off to watch Warrington Town against Mossley in the FA Trophy Preliminary Round. I then had the idea of asking Barry to come to Warrington with us. He is a football fan. At 64, he is more an armchair one than a pitch side one these days, but he enjoys going. I half expected him to decline because he may have felt a sense of duty to stick around at our house with his wife and daughter, so I was pleasantly surprised when he accepted the invite.

On the way from Euxton to Warrington, I updated Barry about Alan's groundhopping activities. 92 League Grounds visited and well over 350 overall but all done without the aid of a driving licence. I also forewarned Barry, a Manchester United fan, that Alan was a passionate City fan.

When Barry and I entered the ground, Barry asked where I had arranged to meet Alan and I said "in the ground".

"Anywhere specifically?" Barry asked, sounding a little concerned.

"Don't worry, Barry, we'll find him. If we head to where they are serving coffee and burgers, we won't go far wrong."

Sure enough, we asked to be pointed in the direction of the canteen and Alan was coming out, coffee in one hand, burger in the other.

"Diet going well, Al!" I said mischievously.

"Cheeky fu##er!" I think was Alan's reply.

I did the introductions and then Barry and I went in to get ourselves a coffee. With going to Spain and having to get my belly out on display for the first time in a long while, the diet that I had kept failing with during the FA Cup campaign has now kicked in properly. I am below fifteen stone for the first time in four years. Thus, I opt out of the usual Snickers/Mars bar/cheeseburger that I would normally have, to complement my coffee. 13 stone 13 pounds was always the aim for the FA Cup Final, I don't think I'll make it for the FA Trophy but perhaps under 14 stone by the FA Vase final 2016 is realistic.

We took our coffees and stood behind the dug outs at the side of the pitch. The ground felt very compact, but has covered areas on three sides, one modern looking stand that could seat about 300 and the famous Cantilever bridge looms over the goal where the home team were warming up. Almost immediately I caught sight of the Warrington Town manager and a sense of familiarity kicked in. I hadn't done my homework, so wasn't aware of who he was, but he was instantly recognisable.

"I know the Warrington Town manager, Alan. Who is he?"

"Don't you know?" Alan replied, knowing the answer was bugging me so dragged the mystery out a little longer.

"No, I know I know him though."

"Family resemblance? Family links to both our clubs?"

"Just tell me."

"Shaun Reid."

"Bloody hell!"

I am an Evertonian, but there is more than just a one sibling link here. Peter Reid may have played for Everton and both managed and played for Manchester City, but it is Shaun Reid's other brother, Michael, that I have closer links to. When I was writing my first book, 'Forever Is Over', I had tried to build up some interest using Twitter and had followed Michael. He followed back, bought 'Forever Is Over' and subsequently bought 'Kiss My Name' and 'Another Saturday & Sweet FA' too. We crossed paths once in a while on Twitter, Michael always doing what he could to support my writing and then one day, he messaged me to say he wanted me to go to the 'Summer School' he was running and present to the girls of Broughton Hall High School in West Derby, Liverpool, where he teaches.

Michael's faith in me was flattering. I had no teaching experience and wasn't initially sure what I was going to do, how I was going to do it and just as importantly who I would be presenting to. I met up with Michael for a beer and to discuss it and it transpires Broughton Hall High School is a Catholic Girls' Secondary School. To ease the new starters in Year Seven into the school, they run a summer school purely for them for two weeks during the summer holidays. It helps the girls get to know some of the teachers and other girls that didn't go to their primary school, find their way around the school without the presence of older children and feel at ease in the new surroundings they will face. To me, it seems like a brilliant idea.

I went along for two days of the two weeks and did presentations to around one hundred girls in a few different sessions. There was a teacher standing in the wings ready to help me out should I find myself struggling but I thoroughly enjoyed it. The only directives I had from Michael was to make it structured and good fun. I did a session on writing stories, but managed to introduce a few modern day themes like Hunger Games, Twilight, One Direction and football. I attempted to persuade them, with the aid of some photoshopped swopping of heads, that I had once been in One Direction and had scored a goal at Goodison Park, but they were having none of it! The feedback from the girls was really positive, the work they did was excellent and I am really grateful to Michael for inviting me along.

There is definitely a family resemblance between all the Reid brothers, but if you have ever seen the fly-on-the-wall documentary made about Sunderland AFC when Peter was manager and then saw Shaun in action on the sidelines at Warrington Town, you would notice the resemblance is not just in looks. Both Michael and Peter's passion for the game and management, is sometimes displayed in four letter language. We stood behind the dugouts for the game and a dire Warrington Town performance was met by a tirade of expletives from Shaun. I text Michael and said I was at Warrington Town and was learning a few new swear words and he text back to say he was surprised it was only a few and by the end of the ninety minutes, it would be plenty!

The language from Shaun Reid even surprised Alan Oliver, no stranger to a foul mouthed rant himself from time to time, but it was more of a shock to the fourth member of our gang of spectators, who had arrived just prior to kick off, Phil Cooper. Phil had been with us for twelve of our fourteen FA Cup Rounds but as a busy solicitor and a single man about town, he had decided there was no way he would be able to better last year's experience, when his side, Arsenal, emerged as winners. Phil is still a novice spectator at non-league level and although occasionally he has been known to utter the odd cursory word himself, he had not experienced anything quite like Shaun Reid before in previous matches. He had only come along, as a friend of Alan's, to bid him well on his FA Trophy campaign, but found himself willing Mossley to win because of Shaun Reid's touchline antics. I could understand Phil's perspective and although Shaun obviously knows his players and we don't, I know a manager giving me a rollicking would have been demotivating to me when I played as I was pretty timid and reacted better to a pat on the back than a kick up the arse. Bad language is not a crime, it doesn't hurt anyone and football is a man's game but used sparingly probably has more impact than when used every sentence. I suppose to an extent we only had ourselves to blame as we had stood directly behind the dugout. If I go to Warrington Town again, I will stand on the other side.

    Having said all that, Warrington Town, prior to this game, were having a good season and as I write (in late November), their season has subsequently become even better because of their FA Cup campaign. Prior to the Warrington-Mossley game, Warrington had played five FA Cup games in three rounds. In the 1st Round Qualifying, they had beaten Trafford 1-0 at home. In the 2nd Qualifying Round they had drawn 0-0 at home to Sheffield, then won 3-1 away in the replay. Then in the 3rd Qualifying Round, they had drawn 1-1 away at Colwyn Bay and, on the Tuesday before our visit to Cantilever Park, had won their replay 1-0 setting up a 4th Round Qualifier with North Ferriby United for a place in the 1st Round Proper.

Perhaps Warrington Town were a little weary from their FA Cup exploits because against Mossley, they were very slow out the blocks and throughout the first half did not manage to up the tempo of their game. After only eight minutes, Mossley took the lead, Andrew Keogh scoring after a goalmouth scramble. That lead was doubled five minutes later when Michael Fish met a cross from the right wing and headed beyond the despairing dive of Warrington Town keeper, Karl Wills.

Warrington had Wills to thank for the score remaining 2-0 at half time as he made a couple of excellent saves, one from a Matt Purcell shot and the other from a cheeky backheel from Michael Fish. In the FA Cup campaign, I mentioned the amount of pop star names the lower league footballers had, this time we had a 1980's weatherman. There was no chance of a hurricane but I'm sure there was an icy blast coming from the Warrington Town dressing room when Shaun Reid got his players in at half time.

During the interval, we headed for a coffee discussing how poor the game had been. Barry had not been to a non-League game for a long time and commented that the quality had been little better than he would see on the local park in Bebington on a Sunday. He was right, Warrington Town were really out of sorts and Mossley had not had to play well to take command. Both sides are in the Evo Stik Division One North, which normally produces a good standard of football, but there can be poor games at every level. Mossley were slightly higher in the table (Mossley 7th, Warrington Town 12th) and their slightly better form and fewer FA Cup battles were perhaps contributory factors in them having the edge.

I also had a read through a very comprehensive programme at half-time. Mossley had been a strong side during the late 1970's/early 1980's and actually reached the FA Trophy Final in 1980 at the old Wembley stadium. There were 26 000 at Wembley to see them fall at the final hurdle, a 2-1 defeat against Dagenham after having been unbeaten in their 30 previous games. I remember a Mossley player called Eamonn O'Keefe playing for Everton, but I think he left Mossley prior to the Wembley final. He never held down a regular place at Goodison Park, but went on to have a good professional career at Wigan Athletic, Port Vale and Blackpool.

I also picked up another interesting fact from the programme. In the early and mid-1960s, Warrington were knocked out the FA Amateur Cup three times by Guinness Exports. My Dad, Richie Wade, played for Guinness for a couple of seasons prior to joining Skelmersdale United, so I checked with him whether he played against Warrington. He said in the 1965-66 season he had played and having beat Warrington Town, Guinness went on to play Skelmersdale United in the next round. This was the game (detailed in 'Another Saturday & Sweet FA'), when my Dad had an altercation with the comedian, Stan Boardman, who was playing for Skelmersdale United at the time and wrongly accused my Dad of stamping. My Dad said "Skem" won 3-2 but Guinness Exports scored an equaliser in injury time which all twenty two players agreed was wrongly ruled out for offside, as the ref and linesman had failed to spot Skelmersdale United's defender, Colin Bridge, standing on the goal line.

The match programme proved more entertaining than the match itself. Once the second half began, the lack of quality that we had witnessed in the first half returned. Mossley sat a bit deeper, encouraging Warrington Town to come at them, but the Mossley keeper, Andrew Farrimond was rarely tested. In the FA Cup, we had been through twelve rounds without a replay but with five minutes left Steve Foster (no relation, as far as I know, to the headbanded Brighton & Hove Albion and Luton

Town skipper of the 1980's) caused a bit of anxiety in our ranks when he set up an interesting finale with a well taken headed goal. Although Foster was not a relation of his legendary namesake, there was one Warrington Town player who did have a more famous sibling. Craig Robinson, Warrington's 32 year old centre back, is the younger brother of MK Dons manager, Karl Robinson.

In injury time, Warrington's captain, David Mannix went close with a free kick, but when referee Michael Ainsworth blew the full time whistle, to signal a 2-1 victory to Mossley, the only man more relieved than Alan Oliver, was the linesman on the touchline next to Shaun Reid, who had endured an entertaining 45 minutes of Shaun Reid rants. As I am sure Shaun would readily admit though, the defeat was not at all down to the officials, it was just down to a poor Warrington Town performance and a creditable Mossley one. Alan checked his phone and discovered New Mills had defeated Ossett Albion, in another all Evo Stik North clash, to set up a New Mills v Mossley tie in the 1st Qualifying Round.

Warrington Town's involvement in our FA Trophy journey was over but their FA Cup campaign was far from finished. On the following Saturday, a much improved performance saw Warrington defeat a strong North Ferriby United side 1-0, in front of a really good crowd of 691, Lewis Field scoring the 66th minute winner. Warrington were then given a plum tie in the FA Cup 1st Round Proper when they were drawn at home to Exeter City and it was selected as the BBC Two live game for Friday 7th November. The BBC have acquired the FA Cup rights back from ITV this year and have been giving their new acquisition some real focus, which has been great for Warrington Town in particular.

Very few people would have given Warrington Town any hope against their League opposition, especially if they had sent spies to the game against Mossley. Warrington were the lowest ranked team left in the competition at the 1st Round Proper stage, but to my astonishment, they were left basking in FA Cup glory as Craig Robinson scored a seventh minute header and they held out for the next 83 minutes to achieve a historic victory for the club and an excellent financial boost too. The tabloids loved the fact that Robinson is a plasterer by trade and I am sure I am not the first to mention that in all likelihood, the Warrington Town players went out and got well and truly plastered after their brilliant victory.

Shaun Reid and his players were then guests of the BBC for the Second Round draw. Warrington Town have been drawn away at Vanarama Conference high flyers, Gateshead, which will again be a televised game in early December. I will make sure I mention the result in the contents of this book. After all their FA Cup exploits so far, it wasn't a great surprise to receive a tweet off Michael Reid recently which simply said, 'I can't believe you chose the Mossley game to watch Warrington'. Alan Oliver has always said he is a jinx and on this occasion, he seems to have been right.

FINAL SCORE : Warrington Town 1 Mossley 2

Saturday 1st November 2014 – FA Trophy 1st Qualifying Round

New Mills v Mossley

Attendance – 152

Since August 2013, when our FA adventures began, the two constants in the 15 Rounds prior to this game, have been Alan and myself. It seems bizarre that from my poolside spot in Calahonda, lazing around in 30 degree heat, I had an urge to be on the terraces at New Mills, in the High Peak area of Derbyshire, on what would no doubt be a cool November day, but once you get on a footballing bandwagon, it seems frustrating when you have to step off. Don't get me wrong, I absolutely loved our first family holiday abroad in four years, it was a welcome tonic, but if Dr.Who could have smuggled me into his Tardis and taken me to New Mills for a couple of hours, then taken me back, that would have been perfect.

The issue I have now, is that once we complete the FA competitions, Cup, Trophy & Vase, I will be annoyed I missed a game. I was hoping for a draw, so I could take some comfort from seeing every round or, at the very least, a New Mills victory, so I could say I saw every side. I said to Alan during the game at Warrington that whichever side emerged victorious from that game was unlikely to progress far but New Mills are struggling towards the foot of the Evo Stik Division One North, so Mossley must have fancied their chances of progressing. With the game being held at New Mills, this looked on paper like the most likely game of the 14 pre-Wembley F.A games we had seen, since the start of last season, to finish in a draw.

Alan does a lot of his groundhopping on his own, but since the start of last season, there had been at least three of us at every FA Cup and FA Trophy game, so it must have seemed a little strange to him, arriving at New Mills without company. Alan isn't afraid to introduce himself to others at the game and before kick off, he began chatting to New Mills Assistant Manager, Paul Armstrong, an ex-FC United of Manchester player. Paul told Alan he wasn't overly confident of victory as some of their first choice players were unavailable.

Paul's lack of optimism was soon proved unfounded as New Mills got off to a flying start. Alan said they came out really fired up and caught Mossley cold. After three minutes, Porya Ahmadi latched on to a Daniel Douglas-Pringle pass and fired home and the lead was doubled three minutes later when Douglas-Pringle added to his assist with a goal of his own. Six minutes in and New Mills were 2-0 up.

Alan is a superstitious soul. He blames Manchester City's thirty odd years of hurt on himself and their recent revival on his absence. Having followed Mossley into this round, he thinks he has jinxed them and his belief gathered momentum in the 15th minute when Ahmadi, the Iranian born striker, who was running the Mossley defence ragged, bagged his second, from a New Mills corner. 3-0.

The score remained 3-0 until half-time, but Alan said New Mills dominance could easily have taken them to the break with a five goal advantage. As Alan headed for his half-time cup of tea, he had a quick word with Paul Armstrong,

"You must be well chuffed, Paul," Alan said.

"Well, I'm glad we got the third as we have a habit of giving two goal leads away this season," was Paul's reply.

Paul Armstrong obviously knows a lot about his team and their propensity to self-destruct ! Mossley came out for the second half re-invigorated and New Mills were on the back foot from the off. It took until the hour mark for Mossley to grab a goal though. Douglas Carroll, the 19 year old striker who had been Mossley's leading goal scorer in 2013-14, made it 3-1. By the 76th minute, it was 3-2, substitute Charlie Anderson, son of the former Nottingham Forest, Manchester United, Arsenal and England full back, Viv Anderson, netted from a goalmouth scramble and set up a tense last fifteen minutes.

During the frantic end to the game, Alan had a text from me in a Calahonda bar! I was desperate to find out how the game was going and when I received a reply saying it was 3-2 to New Mills with ten minutes left, I was hoping Mossley would sneak another one, so we would get our first draw, as I was flying home the following day and could make a midweek replay. New Mills battened down the hatches though and held tight for a 3-2 victory. If it had been a boxing fight, Alan said New Mills would have won on points, although the ref might have stopped it some time during that first half battering. Mossley came close to snatching an equaliser, but New Mills had just about deserved their victory. On the Monday, they would discover where they (and we) would be heading next.

FINAL SCORE :- New Mills 3 Mossley 2

Monday 3rd November 2014

Having not been abroad for four years, it was a reality check arriving back in Manchester at 11pm on Sunday night and then being back in work on Monday morning, but there was at least a little solace in knowing the FA Trophy draw was taking place at midday and we would discover where we would be heading to next. If New Mills were to be drawn at home, it would give me the opportunity to see their ground and if they were drawn away, there was a strong chance it would be somewhere new for me (although perhaps not for Alan who by this point had clocked up over 360 grounds).

Just after midday, I had a text off Alan that simply said,

"Mickleover Sports, away - that's Derby mate."

Straight away this had my buy-in. In the FA Cup adventure, I had visited seven grounds that were new to me and having missed a trip to New Mills, Mickleover Sports and a trip to the other side of Derbyshire seemed very tempting indeed. I was up for this and having missed one game, I knew the old enthusiasm was back. I was going to be Alan's FA Trophy wingman and if I couldn't get to every round, I was keen to make sure I could go to as many as I possibly could, starting at Mickleover Sports in the Second Qualifying Round.

Saturday 15th November 2014 – FA Trophy 2nd Qualifying Round

Mickleover Sports v New Mills

Attendance – 204

Picking Alan Oliver up from Buckshaw Parkway train station on a Saturday morning and then heading off to a random English football ground has become a bit of a habit over the last twelve months, so there was definitely a 'Groundhog Day' feeling when this was repeated once more for our trip to Mickleover. Last season, these trips usually involved Alan's daughter, Jordan, his mate, Phil Cooper or my Dad (or any combination of the three), so it did seem a little different that this time it was just going to be Alan and me.

There was plenty to catch up on, so the two hour car journey passed quickly. One of the things we discussed was how a few of the players that we had watched during last year's FA Cup had moved clubs and were making sporting headlines elsewhere. I had noted that Luke Freeman, the Stevenage midfielder, who had been one of the players that had impressed me the most on our travels, had moved to Bristol City and had been earning rave reviews and scoring plenty of goals during their impressive start to their Division One campaign. Freeman is definitely a Championship quality player and if Bristol City's good form continues, he may well get the chance to prove it next season.

Alan had spotted another equally interesting move. Danny Johnson, Guisborough Town's impressive striker, had gone on to score a massive 59 goals in all competitions in the 2013-14 season, including the only goal in the North Riding Senior Cup Final against Middlesbrough. This impressive tally earned him a number of awards, including the Northern League's 'Young Player of The Year' award, it also captured the attention of several League clubs and Johnson opted to sign for Championship side, Cardiff City. Johnson played for Cardiff's development squad during their pre-season tour and had scored in their game against FK Sarajevo, but perhaps feeling he was not quite ready for the Championship, Cardiff loaned Johnson out to Tranmere Rovers in October and on Tuesday night, he had scored his first professional goal, for Tranmere, in their 2-1 Football League Trophy victory over Bury. Both Freeman and Johnson are young players to keep an eye out for in the coming seasons.

Mickleover is a village two miles West of Derby but it has a rural rather than suburban feel. Passing through in the car, it appears to be a prosperous area, with several attractive pubs, which would have appealed to me, if I wasn't just there for a few hours to witness a football match. Apparently, when the new Wembley was being built and the English football team played their games in various locations up and down the country, Mickleover Court Hotel had the England team as their guests prior to the England-Mexico friendly at Pride Park, Derby, in 2001.

Alan and I arrived at the Mickleover Sports Raygar Stadium before two and my car was the first in the small car park next to the road. We did our obligatory entrance photographs and were greeted by friendly stewards on the turnstile, which immediately gave me the impression that it was a warm, hospitable club. Both Alan and myself always buy programmes and raffle tickets from our host club and the raffle seller was a friendly old chap with a faltering memory, who could remember the prize was a bottle of whiskey but could not recall what brand. I'm not keen on whiskey and Alan is teetotal, so if we had won, we would probably have given it back for the next game.

We wandered into the clubhouse, which may well double up as the clubhouse for the neighbouring cricket club too. Portsmouth were on the TV in there, playing away at Plymouth Argyle and I grimaced when I noticed they were 3-0 down. I regularly go to watch Pompey as my wife Alison's Uncle Dereck and cousins Tom and Ben are big fans. Earlier this season, I took my eldest son, Brad with Dereck and Ben to see them lose at Stoke City in the Capital One Cup. Their fans, as always, were fantastic and it is always the fans that are made to suffer for boardroom irregularities. There had been a glimmer of hope that this may turn out to be a good season for Pompey, but after a good start, there were already signs that a promotion push may be beyond them. They should be a Championship side at the very least.

As I headed towards the bar, I noticed the majority of the people in there, were lads aged around sixteen to eighteen, clad in Academy Team tracksuits, accompanied by their devoted parents. When I was a child, most parents just dropped their kids off at the park, but thankfully this seems to have changed and more fathers and especially more mothers tend to go to watch their children now. Most of the Mickleover parents seemed to be just having a quick sandwich and heading home before the afternoon first team match kicked off, but some did stay to witness the main event.

I bought myself a pint of the local draught bitter called 'Sweet Sixteen' and Alan a glass of coke from the bar. Apparently the bitter was introduced to commemorate Mickleover Sports sixteen consecutive victories in the 2009-10 season and very pleasant it was too. Having supped up, we wandered outside to have a look around the ground. Alan had been before, but we have both developed an interest in walking around the ground before kick off and taking a photograph from a corner flag.

It isn't actually possible to wander around the whole of Raygar Stadium as only three and a half sides are terraced. The side that backs on to the cricket pitch has a small standing area at the far end (away from the clubhouse which is behind the goal), so we began to walk as far as we could go. We only managed to get to the corner flag at the clubhouse end before being distracted by the smell of coffee and burgers from the van in the corner. The chalkboard displayed a "Two Chicken Burgers for £3 Special" which immediately grabbed Alan's attention and he swiftly put his order in. When one bun with two chicken burgers inside was handed over, his face dropped a little, but once he had devoured it, he was glad there hadn't been a second bun.

Having been fed and watered, we took our corner flag photographs and positioned ourselves on the far side of the pitch, opposite the Main Stand, as far around as the barriers would allow us to go. I watched the New Mills young keeper warming up and took a few mental notes, as my eldest son, 14 year old, Brad, is a goalkeeper and I could do with a few different drills for his pre-match warm ups. After watching the goalkeeper, my attention turned to the three officials warm up and the middle one of the three, was a woman. The referee tends to warm up in the middle of the two assistants, so this was going to be a first for me. I had seen several ladies run the line at this level, but not referee. I checked my programme and sure enough the ref was named as Lisa Rashid.

Fifteen minutes later the game was under way. Within the first ten seconds, a New Mills player, possibly testing the female ref, leapt into a tackle with some real ferocity and he was dragged away from the rest of the players for an early ticking off. Alan had already mentioned how New Mills had started their last Round game at pace and they were keen to do the same this time. There was a bit of back chat to the ref, but she handled it calmly although I did find it amusing that at one stage she urged the players to "be careful", something they blatantly did not appear keen to do.

There was no doubting she was a competent official though and it appeared it only took a few minutes for the players to accept this fact.

We had not been able to get a team sheet prior to kick off, so we were using our programmes to get some idea who was who. New Mills had a striker on their books called Matt Landregan, who had played for and scored for Radcliffe Borough when they lost 2-1 at Burscough in our FA Cup journey last season. He didn't appear to be in the first eleven though. Alan recognised the New Mills left back called Danny Caldecott, who he had seen play many times for Ashton United and knew several of the New Mills players from the previous round, but with the Mickleover Sports team we were identifying them by shouts from the terraces or player interaction.

Mickleover Sports are in the Evostik South, New Mills are in Evostik North. Mickleover are towards the top of their League and New Mills towards the bottom of theirs. Both Leagues are meant to be of an equal standing and Mickleover had won eight home games out of eight in the League, so everything pointed towards a Mickleover victory, but despite Mickleover looking like the better footballing side, New Mills looked up for a footballing battle and it came as no great surprise when New Mills took an early lead, Poya Ahmadi, New Mills Iranian striker scoring after a pacey run culminated in a neat finish.

As the half progressed, Mickleover were gradually beginning to dominate proceedings. Everything seemed to be going through their playmaker in central midfield, captain, Liam Walshe who had formerly played for Stafford Rangers. Despite their dominance, Mickleover rarely called New Mills keeper, Aaron Ashley, into action. I subsequently discovered young Ashley was a debutant, having recently joined New Mills from Rochdale. His basic handling appeared good, he was very quick off his line and he kicked a ball very well, perhaps what led to his departure from Rochdale was a lack of a physical presence, as he appeared less than six feet tall. At half-time a potential clean sheet was still on the cards, as New Mills went into the break maintaining their one goal advantage.

In the ten minutes or so preceding Miss Rashid's half time whistle, it had gone noticeably colder. There was also a cold mist that was starting to descend. Alan and I decided to wander back over to the van by the corner flag to get something to warm us up. Alan had already spotted that they sold homemade minestrone soup, so we queued up only to discover that others had beaten us to the soup and we had to settle for coffee. The gloom over the ground seemed to be getting worse. I looked around, there were only four small floodlights in the corners of the ground, that didn't seem to be lighting the whole of the pitch up or cutting through what could now be described as 'fog' rather than 'mist'.

Alan spotted me looking up to the heavens.

"You don't think there's any chance that this game...."

"Don't even say it," Alan cut in, knowing exactly what I was about to say.

A midweek 190 mile round trip didn't exactly appeal to either of us. At least if the game finished level, which wouldn't have surprised me as Mickleover were likely to raise their game in the second half, the replay at New Mills would have then been on the right side of Derbyshire for us.

When we returned to the same vantage point to watch the second half, we noticed two other men had arrived besides us. Alan began to chat to them about his groundhopping exploits and it transpired they were formerly the management team at Coalville Town for eight years. Modesty prevented them from saying it, but during their tenure, Adam Stevens and his Assistant had led the club to Wembley to an FA Vase final in 2011, where they lost 3-2 to Whitley Bay. I have subsequently watched the highlights on FATV and it appears Coalville were unlucky, twice coming from behind to equalise, hitting the woodwork twice and the Whitley Bay keeper also made some tremendous saves. Both Stevens and his assistant seemed like good blokes but did give the impression they would not suffer fools gladly and I could imagine they were not afraid to adopt the Shaun Reid style of management when necessary!

As the players came out for the second half, Adam Stevens agreed with me that the floodlights were struggling to keep the pitch lit with the fog making it ever more difficult to see all the players.

"Might be an idea to call this off," Stevens commented.

"Technically, if you can see both goals from the halfway line, then it is fit to play," I replied, putting my knowledge gleaned from the 'You Are The Ref' section of Shoot Magazine from my childhood to good use.

"I know, mate," Stevens replied, "but from a spectator's point of view and from a player safety perspective, they shouldn't be playing in this."

Miss Rashid saw fit to start the second half, however and Mickleover Sports again began to exert their authority, orchestrated by the very useful Liam Walshe. From our vantage point, it was difficult to see where the ball was set to land from goal kicks and also not too easy to see the far side of the pitch. I had pointed out to Alan in the first half that one of the four bulbs on one of the four floodlights had gone, so the visibility in one corner wasn't as good and, as mentioned, the central areas were poorly lit. The game reminded me of playing football with my mates down at the park, in my summer holidays, as a kid and continuing to play as dusk fell, when it was hard to make out who had the ball.

I guess in the back of Miss Rashid's mind, was the added complication that New Mills were holding on to a 1-0 lead. The New Mills players and management staff would not be too happy about an abandonment when they could be on the verge of one of their biggest wins of the season. This complication was removed in the 56th minute. Chris Palmer floated across a free kick that was met on the far post by Dwayne Wiley, who struck a low, hard volley past a helpless Aaron Ashley and into the back of the New Mills net. 1-1.

With Mickleover Sports on top, it looked like there were only two possible winners now, Mickleover or the weather. The players seemed to be relatively happy with conditions and were continuing without protest to Lisa Rashid and her assistants, but the fog was not clearing at all and ten minutes after the equaliser, Rashid blew her full-time whistle to indicate the match was abandoned.

"Correct decision, she could have just abandoned it at half-time," commented former Coalville Town boss, Stevens.

"Flippin' heck," said Alan, and if you know him, you know that's not quite what he said, "we'll have to come back for the flippin' re-arranged match. We need to find out when that is."

Alan was trying to give off the impression that he was gutted by the abandonment but in reality, I suddenly realised he was chuffed to bits with it. In fourteen FA Cup rounds, we had avoided any major incidents and although it was a challenge trekking all over the country, it could have been made far more difficult by replays hundreds of miles away. A draw between Doncaster Rovers and Stevenage, for example, in the 3rd Round in January, could have seen us doing a 400 plus mile round trip on a cold winter's Tuesday or Wednesday night. I think deep down, Alan was wanting more of a challenge and already the FA Trophy had provided us with our first midweek game. The stewards at Mickleover confirmed the replay would be on Tuesday and this was soon confirmed by the gentleman operating the tannoy system.

From my own perspective, I must admit, I was hiding an inner pleasure about the abandoned match too. There are worse places than Mickleover Sports to have to return to. The pitch is great, the atmosphere is incredibly warm and friendly, the team play good football and I enjoyed the rarity of watching a female referee attempting to control twenty two young men (and in this case succeeding). I presumed she would be asked to officiate again on the Tuesday night re-arranged game. A ninety minute drive wasn't too bad either. Furthermore, it was the Mickleover fog that persuaded me that there was a book in this journey and it was well worth me accompanying Alan in every round of the FA Trophy trail.

For several weeks, I had debated whether there was much of a story to be told by going to every round of the FA Trophy. The FA Cup is loved by millions and tales are often recounted about its magic, but the FA Trophy does not excite non-League football fans like its big brother. There are no trips to Old Trafford or the

Emirates at the end of this rainbow and the pots of gold that come with TV deals with BBC or BT Sports aren't there either.

Conference sides only enter the competition in the First Round Proper and if a Conference side wins the FA Trophy, their total prize money from the Football Association equates to £92 000. As a lot of the Conference sides are now professional, this is not a huge sum of money. Getting through a few rounds for the likes of Mickleover Sports or New Mills, however, is a bit of a godsend. They are only semi-professional and three or four wins can pay their wage bill for a good portion of the season. Relative to the FA Cup though, the money is peanuts. Each team that is televised in the FA Cup Third Round receives £144 000 plus they receive an additional £67 500 from the FA prize fund if they win. Thus, if a Conference side, for example, makes it to the FA Cup Third Round and then receives a plum tie, they are laughing all the way to the bank. It isn't all about the money though and the FA Trophy represents a rare opportunity for players at semi-professional or lower professional level to play at Wembley and for their club to win a major trophy. From a writer's perspective, being realistic, I am unlikely to attract as much of an audience writing about the FA Trophy, as I was writing about the FA Cup. I have had to decide whether it is a story worth telling at all. Three rounds in, I have decided the book may only ever have a 'cult' interest, but events are already conspiring to ensure that it is a story worth writing.

"FINAL" SCORE :- Mickleover Sports 1 New Mills 1

MATCH ABANDONED AFTER 65 MINUTES

Monday 17th November 2014 – FA Trophy 3rd Qualifying Round Draw

Due to Saturday's abandonment, both Mickleover Sports and New Mills were in the hat for the draw for the next round. The draw for each round takes place at midday on the Monday following Saturday's previous round games, but it takes about half an hour to update on the 'FA' website, so we have tended to find out where we are heading next from Twitter updates from the club we are following. This time around, we could use both Mickleover Sports and New Mills twitter sites for up to the minute news.

At five past twelve, my mobile phone rang, it was Alan.

"North Ferriby United, away, mate," Alan announced.

"OK," I had heard of them, they are in Chorley's League, but my geographical knowledge of their location was limited, "whereabouts is that, Alan?"

"Hull, mate. The ground is in the shadows of the Humber Bridge."

When Alan and I had been chatting through where we could possibly head to for the next round, on Saturday, every time he mentioned a team, I would reply by saying I have a friend who lives near there.

"You know what I am going to say, Alan, don't you?"

"You have a friend who lives near there."

"Exactly!"

In this instance, it was a very good friend. Jamie Lowe, Skegness born, but a resident of Hull for twenty years. We had been to Manchester Poly together, meeting in Halls of Residence in Didsbury and then spending three drunken years together.

In 'Another Saturday & Sweet FA', I mentioned that Jamie was one of the lads I drunkenly stumbled on to the beach with for a night's sleep, prior to being mugged at knifepoint in Tenerife. Jamie is such a nice guy he makes Gary Lineker seem like Adolf Hitler. We still see each other regularly but because of family life, not as often as I would like, but this FA Trophy draw now provided us with an opportunity to meet up. From a personal perspective, it was a great draw.

Tuesday 18th November 2014 – FA Trophy 2nd Qualifying Round (Take Two)

Mickleover Sports v New Mills

Attendance – 88

Alan Oliver has regularly made a Saturday morning train journey from Manchester Piccadilly to Buckshaw Parkway, but for the first time ever, he had to join commuters on the trip, as we prepared for our first midweek adventure in our FA travels. The logistics of doing a midweek trip are never going to be simple, but mine were compounded by having an incredibly hard working wife who works shifts as a Midwife and two Secondary school age sons who are very sporty.

Tuesday is not normally a busy sports night for our family, as Monday, Wednesday, Friday, Saturday and Sunday are the days of the week that involve our children's sports events. Joel, my twelve year old youngest son, had, however, been picked to play for the school basketball team, so after work and prior to driving to Mickleover, I had to collect him from school. Alison, my wife, was due home from her hospital shift at about nine o'clock, so I needed to give Joel and Brad their 'tea' before heading off. I cheated and bought them a rare 'chippy tea', so once they were tucking in, Alan and I departed for Mickleover's Raygar Stadium once more.

With regards to my work, I am still working at 'World of Warranty' where I started in October 2013, when my financial situation was at its most desperate. This job is unlikely to make me rich, but it does help me pay every bill every month and I have gradually caught up on any payments that were behind. In the long-term, I think I would like to return to the financial services sector, but for now, I am just trying to do as good a job as I can. I know very little about cars, so it has been a learning process from day one, but no-one at the company is vindictive or has a deceitful manner, so it is a much improved environment to my latter days at my previous PAYE role at Lloyds Bank.

On the way, Alan and I discussed the best way to get him back home. There seemed no point in him coming all the way back to Buckshaw with me and getting the train back into Manchester, so I was thinking of stations I could drop him off at. I knew Alan had been speaking to New Mills Assistant Manager, Paul Armstrong at the game against Mossley and Al mentioned Paul had been in touch on Twitter asking him if he wanted a lift to the game on the team coach, which he had turned down because we had already made arrangements to meet up. I suggested Alan should contact Paul to see if he could get a lift back on their coach after the game.

"Great idea, Cal. I can't see them bringing many supporters, so there's bound to be spare seats and most of the lads are from Manchester, so they may even pass Failsworth on the way back. I'll send Paul a message on Twitter."

Paul Armstrong subsequently replied saying there was loads of room and he was more than welcome to jump on, after the game. Non-League clubs and the people who watch their games have a close bond and this small act of generosity was a good indication of this. I can't see many Premier League teams opening their coach doors to a stranded supporter! It may happen, but I would guess not very often.

We were a bit concerned that M6 traffic could delay our arrival in Mickleover but we arrived by seven. We parked up on the small car park at the road side and headed up the pathway towards the ground. As we headed to the entrance turnstile, Alan spotted the New Mills coach parked outside the entrance and gathered pace as he spotted Paul Armstrong sitting at the front. Alan knocked on the window and beckoned for Paul to come out, which he did.

"How's it going, mate?" Alan said shaking Paul's hand with a firm Mancunian grip.

"Good. Good."

"You just got here?"

"No, been here about half an hour. Took a while with the traffic, but loads of time."

"How come you're not inside with the lads? I thought you'd be out on the pitch with them." Alan asked.

"Erm, I just let them out and they went in themselves."

"Oh, right. Thanks very much for this, by the way, really good of you. Twitter came in handy there."

Alan was given a confused look.

"You don't recognise me, do you?" Alan said.

"Yeh, I do, but I'm not sure where from mate."

"I'm Alan, you saw me at the Mossley game. Said on Twitter you'd give me a lift back after the game."

"Hang on. Who do you think I am?"

Now Alan looked puzzled.

"You're Paul Armstrong, New Mills Assistant Manager.

"No, I'm not mate. I'm the bus driver!"

Cue laughter and a relieved bus driver who said he was trying for the life of him to think how he knew Alan.

After the mistaken identity, we headed into the Raygar Stadium, a grand sounding title for a relatively small ground. We had plenty of time to buy a programme and visit the van in the corner to buy something to eat and a homemade Minestrone Soup each that we had missed out on, in the previous game. Disappointingly, a quick flick through the programme revealed that other than the date change on the cover, the contents were exactly the same as Saturday's! I guess it was worth £2 just for the novelty value.

Having eaten our burgers and polished off our soup, we headed to the bar and Alan spotted the real Paul Armstrong in there, having a quick pre-match drink. On the TV, they were previewing the Scotland-England friendly that was due to kick off. The fact that the international match was live on TV was probably a factor in the crowd at Mickleover looking like it was going to be far less than it had been on Saturday. England had beaten Slovenia 3-1 on Saturday to maintain their 100% record in their European Championship Qualifying Group, but Alan was convinced it was a stupid idea to play the Scots in a friendly in their own back yard and a real whipping was on the cards for England.

Paul Armstrong came across as a guy with a good heart but a short fuse. He was a former FC United of Manchester player who knew a lot of the local non-League players, as did Alan, so they had a good chat about some mutual acquaintances. Paul confessed his temper had got the better of him during New Mills recent poor run and he was serving a three match touchline ban for an altercation with a referee after their game away at Farsley when he had gone into the officials changing room and used abusive language. He felt that with players missing through injury and work commitments for this hastily arranged fixture, New Mills would struggle to get anything out of the game. I couldn't disagree with him, Mickleover Sports had looked like the better side on Saturday and I was fully expecting them to get through to the next round.

After our drink in the bar, we headed around three sides of the ground to the same spot we had stood at for Saturday's game. Other than the fact it was a night game, there was a déjà vu feeling, as the floodlights were on, the same teams were doing their pre-match warm ups and the officials were the same too, with Lisa Rashid and her two Assistant Referees. Once the game kicked off, the match itself followed a similar pattern too, with New Mills coming out of the blocks quickly and taking the upper hand in the early battles.

It had only taken New Mills two minutes to make the breakthrough on Saturday, but this time it took 35 minutes for their superiority to become a mathematical one. Midfielder Ryan Hopper striking a shot that Mickleover Sports keeper, Chris Martin, managed to get a hand to but couldn't keep out. Chris Martin, the latest in a long line of players we have come across on our FA travels who shares his name with a pop star, this time Coldplay's lead singer, has a thick set frame and suits their style of play as he distributes the ball brilliantly with his feet, but in the 100 minutes of football we have seen him in, has yet to convince me he is the best shot stopper at this level.

"Great name that," Alan commented.

"Chris Martin?" I asked.

"No, no, the goalscorer, Ryan Hopper!"

"Any relation?" I asked with a smile.

"A distant cousin."

Going a goal down seemed to wake the Mickleover Sports team out of their early malaise. They lifted their game and I commented to Alan that New Mills needed to get in at half-time with a lead. Try as we might to remain neutral, Alan and I often find we have leanings towards one of the teams. As Alan had followed New Mills into the round, was getting a lift back off them and knew their Assistant Manager, his slight leaning was towards them. I had put £2 on a midweek football accumulator, which included England to beat Scotland and Mickleover Sports to beat New Mills, so I was quietly hoping for a Mickleover come back.

On the stroke of half time, Mickleover Sports scored an all important equaliser. A ball was flighted over and Aaron Ashley, the New Mills keeper, probably the only man in footballing history to make his debut twice (as the abandoned first game on Saturday will not be counted in the record books) seemed to collect the ball and then lose it, but dazzled by the floodlights, Alan and I couldn't quite see whether he just lost his grip or was fouled by the Mickleover Sports attacker. As mentioned on Saturday, he isn't the tallest of keepers, so the physical side of goalkeeping is probably not his strongest attribute. As the ball broke free, it was bundled over the line by the elaborately named Mickleover Sports forward, Nico DeGirolamo.

New Mills protests were led by Danny Caldecott, but Lisa Rashid was heard to say the keeper did not have full control of the ball. The half time whistle blew soon after, so we headed to the burger van once again, asking other spectators on our way what their view of the equaliser was. The general consensus was that it could easily have been given as a foul as the ball was headed out of Aaron Ashley's hands. Having been at the 1984 FA Cup Final between Everton and Watford, as an Evertonian, I had not complained when something similar happened between Andy Gray and Watford keeper, Steve Sherwood, but I did feel a little sorry for young Ashley who was no doubt very keen to make a good impression on his second debut.

Having grabbed a coffee, we decided to head over to the Sports bar to see how England were doing. Alan was surprised and I was pleased to note that they were leading 1-0. Paul Armstrong, came back into the bar, his three match touchline ban had kept him out of the dugout and the dressing room, so it gave us an opportunity to have a chat with him. He wasn't too vehement in his protests about the equaliser, I could imagine he would be a tough player and would have little sympathy for minor infringements on a goalkeeper.

The second half started fairly equally and for a few minutes we started to think we could have our first replay and our first abandonment in the same round. Mickleover Sports rely less on hard work and more on the technical aspects of the game than New Mills though and their superior footballing ability began to show. A break down the left lead to a ball pulled back from the by line which allowed Jordan Bell the simplest of tap ins. 2-1. For another thirty minutes, Mickleover Sports remained on the front foot and Aaron Ashley had to make a number of good saves to prevent New Mills going two goals down.

Sensing victory, with a few minutes to go, Mickleover Sports began to drop deeper and New Mills pushed men forward seeking an equaliser that would take the game in to extra time. This always carried a risk that New Mills may be caught on the break by the quick Mickleover Sports forwards and this is how things transpired. In injury time, Shaquille Antoine-Clarke had a rasping shot for New Mills deflected for a corner and as the corner was cleared, Mickleover Sports players surged forward against a New Mills defence that was down to a couple of men. A through ball to Andy Dales allowed him time to advance on goal and he beat Ashley in the New Mills goal with aplomb. 3-1 to Mickleover Sports and they would be making the trip to North Ferriby United.

Within seconds of Mickleover's third goal, Lisa Rashid blew the final whistle. The Mickleover Sports – New Mills fixture had provided a lot to write about. An abandonment, an excellent female ref, a player who may go down in history for making his debut twice, a warm welcome (twice over) and six goals. I headed for the exit and Alan headed across to meet up with Paul Armstrong and the rest of the New Mills players and staff who would be heading home despondently. Alan later told me Paul Armstrong not only arranged for him to get on the coach, he also drove Alan back home to Failsworth afterwards. He said we would be welcome to go to New Mills later in the season as his guests, something I would be keen to do, as currently New Mills is the missing piece in my FA jigsaw.

Incidentally, despite England winning 3-1 against Scotland, with Wayne Rooney scoring his 45th and 46th England goals and Mickleover Sports defeating New Mills, I still lost on my £2 accumulator. New Saints failed to beat Port Talbot at home, finishing 0-0 despite New Saints being 13-2 on (ie. If you put £13 on, you would win £2!). A fool and his money are easily parted.

FINAL SCORE :- Mickleover Sports 3 New Mills 1

Saturday 29th November 2014 – FA Trophy 3rd Qualifying Round

North Ferriby United v Mickleover Sports

Attendance – 220

There is a sign in our hallway that I bought Alison one Christmas that reads, "Remember, as far as everyone else is aware, we are nice, normal family."

Our boys, Brad and Joel, are fourteen and twelve respectively now and despite being well behaved at school and in public places, they are a nightmare, at times, at home. Brad is almost six feet tall and if Joel does anything, no matter how minor, to irritate him, he likes nothing better than to give him a punch in the arm or chest. You would think Joel would learn to keep away, but instead he goes looking for trouble and very few days pass without some sort of incident. After a Friday evening of name calling, punching, kicking, shouting and running around the house like wild things, I decided it would not be safe to leave them to their own devices whilst I went to the game and Alison was working. So, as the youngest and maddest, Joel was told he had to come with me to North Ferriby. He was not amused.

90% of the time, I get on very well with both our boys. Brad is full of self-confidence and is intelligent, sporty, good looking and quick witted. He is also selfish, stubborn and lazy! Joel is quieter, very regimented, a little immature, sporty, hard working and generous but with an uncontrollable temper. As a father, I would say I am always there for them, but sometimes when I am there, I am short tempered, irritable and as stubborn as Brad. I am sure they will both grow up to be decent men, I just sometimes wish the journey to adulthood wasn't along such a bumpy road.

Since September, Joel has found himself a job as a paper boy. At first, as we enjoyed another Indian summer, he would go off on his bike and he would only phone me if he was struggling to complete the round before school, so I could meet him and deliver a few papers. Once the weather turned though, I started to drive him around on the wet and windy days. This has somehow become every day. To be fair to Joel though, I am merely his assistant. He always goes into the paper shop and sorts the papers out, delivers the majority of the papers and very rarely struggles to get himself out of bed. We do seven days a week and he always offers me a cut of his wages. As I refuse to accept anything, a couple of weeks ago, he went to Tesco and bought me a coffee machine.

On this particular morning, Joel was not in a good mood. He goes to bed too late for his early morning starts and as he likes his routine, the fact that he was being made to get in the car at half past ten and go to North Ferriby, a place he had never heard of, visiting friends of mine he did not know, only added to his grumpy manner. When Alan clambered cheerily into the car at Buckshaw Parkway, Joel did not return his greetings. A few years ago, I would have given Joel a telling off for being rude, but I have learnt that telling him off only prolongs his mood and the best thing to do is to just ignore him.

On the way over to North Ferriby, I phoned Jamie on my mobile (hands free) to confirm our arrival at his house at about quarter to one. Jamie lives in Brough, about three miles from North Ferriby. His personal life over the last few years has returned to normality after a turbulent period that was like something out of Kramer versus Kramer. He had to cope with a marital split and his ex-wife and subsequently his daughter moving to Cardiff, but over time he bounced back, met his second wife, Amy and they now have a young son together, as well as three daughters between them. Jamie's daughter was staying with them for the weekend and as she was up to celebrate her 13th birthday, Jamie explained that he would be unable to come to the game but would come to the next one if North Ferriby United won and subsequently had another home draw. As they are a couple of Leagues higher up the pyramid than Mickleover Sports, North Ferriby would be the more likely winners, so it was probably 50-50 that we would be back.

After an hour's stop off at Jamie's in Brough, filling our stomachs with sausage barmcakes and having a good catch up with Jamie and Amy, we headed over to North Ferriby. Jamie works for a company that sells confectionery, so Joel came out of his bad mood a little when Jamie handed him a big bag of sweets. Alan had been to North Ferriby's 'EON Visual Media Stadium' before, so advised that there was a narrow passageway leading up to the ground, so it was best to park on the main road, by the allotments and walk up. We were there just after two and it was very quiet, so we parked right next to the passageway and headed in.

There are similarities between Mickleover and North Ferriby, as both grounds are situated in pleasant suburban areas. Some of the houses we passed on our route into North Ferriby were enormous and led to a string of questions from Joel about whether a footballer lived in them. Alan and I did not know, but would not have been surprised. Rumour had it that Steve Bruce, Hull City's manager, lived locally and would often wander down to watch North Ferriby if their games did not clash with Hull's. As they are situated in a village, they have one of the smaller average gates in the Conference North, but presumably, if they went on an FA Trophy run, the supporters from Hull City may start to come down too.

We started this FA Trophy adventure at Warrington and co-incidentally Warrington knocked North Ferriby United out of this year's FA Cup, 1-0, so North Ferriby United may well have learnt about the dangers of underestimating lower League opposition. Having seen both Mickleover Sports and Warrington Town already, we knew they carry a different type of threat, with Warrington being a more combative side and Mickleover Sports looking dangerous going forward at pace.

Once we were in the stadium, we did our usual lap of the ground and corner flag photos, which Joel avoided. The pitch slopes slightly from one side to the other, with the lower side, on the far side of the ground, having a long stand, which is about eight rows deep, that runs from one goalmouth to the other, with roofed terracing in each corner. The other three sides are terraced, but the near side is sloping and slightly elevated above pitch level, so we decided this was the best vantage point.

Prior to kick off, we had a brief chat with Mickleover Sports media representative, Phil Matthews, who Alan had met earlier in the season, when he had seen Mickleover win 3-1 away at Tividale. We had also seen Phil at the two games at Mickleover's Raygar Stadium. Anyway, he explained that he strongly suspected this would be the end of the line for Mickleover, as they had a few regulars missing including their centre forward, Karl Ashton who had gone on holiday with his girlfriend. It seemed very strange to me and Alan that a semi-professional footballer would book his holiday in the middle of the football season, but I guess the club are powerless to stop him.

To try to plug the gap left by Karl Ashton, Mickleover Sports manager, Glenn Kirkwood, has been in touch with his ex-boss from his playing days at Burton Albion, Nigel Clough. Clough is now manager at Sheffield United and has loaned Mickleover

Sports, Chris Hamilton, a quick attacker who plays on the right. It would be expecting a lot for Hamilton to slot straight in though, but Mickleover Sports main focus is their League campaign in the Evo Stik First Division South, so this might be a good time for him to be blooded. Mickleover have been further in this year's FA Trophy than ever before and although they must enjoy picking up the cheques for progressing, they realistically know they are very unlikely to win it.

Once the game kicked off, the lack of expectation from Phil Matthews was not matched by the Mickleover Sports players in the first fifteen minutes. Despite North Ferriby United being a much bigger side, with a giant of a centre forward called Tom Denton causing all sorts of problems for the much smaller Mickleover Sports centre backs, it was hard to decipher who were the Conference North side. Mickleover Sports were spraying the ball around and looking confident. Mickleover's early good work was undone though, in the 17th minute, when a cross from the left wing was met by Tom Denton on the far post and he used his aerial strength to head home.

It is hard to avoid clichés when writing about Tom Denton as he is an old fashioned centre forward in a young man's body. Denton must be 6 feet 5 inches tall, is strong physically, a build more like a rugby number eight than Peter Crouch, but is slow around the field but dynamite in the air. One of my favourite comments from Joe Royle was when he said about his snailed paced, Oldham Athletic centre forward, Ron Futcher, "if he'd have just been slow, he'd have been brilliant." This could equally apply to Denton. At this level though, he was almost impossible to play against and North Ferriby United were happy to either pump their goal kicks towards him or get it to their wide men and loop crosses over for him to latch on to. A poor man's Andy Carroll would be an accurate description.

Having taken the lead, North Ferriby United were thankful for a really poor decision by the referee and his assistant stood in line with the North Ferriby United left back. Mickleover Sports were attacking and a bouncing ball was played to debutant Chris Hamilton on their right. His first touch controlled the ball, but it bounced back up to waist height. Out of nowhere, North Ferriby United's centre back, Matt Wilson sprinted across and dived two footed into a tackle that was chest high. The incident occurred right in front of us and it almost felt like we should take cover as he flew through the air like Superman, but with his boots rather than his arms leading the way. Wilson connected with some of the ball and some of the man, in a tackle the likes of which is normally only seen in black and white footage of football between the wars.

"I got the ball ref, I got the ball!" Wilson protested.

"He's off!" Alan, Joel and I whispered to each other in tones quiet enough to avoid Wilson hearing. He didn't look like the type of man you would pick a fight with. Perhaps the referee and his Assistant also had self-preservation at the heart of their decision making, as they pleaded temporary blindness and gave a throw in to Mickleover. To add insult to injury, Wilson was booked later in the half for another clumsy challenge and the North Ferriby United bench were out on their feet to protest. In reality though, I think they realised he had been incredibly fortunate to last 45 minutes without seeing red and when the players returned for the second half, Wilson had been substituted. Chatting to North Ferriby supporters at half-time, they explained it was not an isolated incident and he had only been back a few games from a previous suspension, after he was sent off for an off the ball incident at Warrington Town. Earlier in the season, he was the club captain, so he is no doubt a leader on the pitch, but from the evidence in the first half, he needs to find the balance between competitiveness and recklessness.

During the half-time break, Joel, aided by a hot chocolate and a bar of chocolate, became spritely and talkative, as if he had finally accepted where he was and was actually enjoying it. He was chatting away to Alan about all the grounds he had visited and spotted a 20p piece by the touchline, which he wanted to vault over the barrier to get to, but I wouldn't let him. Joel does actually enjoy going to different places and doing different things, he just doesn't like the idea of it. Alan said if his punishments as a child were being dragged to football matches, he would have been delighted.

Despite breaking Wade family tradition and supporting Manchester United rather than Everton (Alison's Dad is a United fan), Joel has seen Everton win every game he has been to and always seems to go to exciting games, for example, he was at Everton's 7-1 demolition of Sunderland a few years back and also went to Everton's first win at Craven Cottage for over 30 years. He brought his good fortune to North Ferriby, as the second half turned out to be a cracker.

Mickleover Sports hard work, good football and endeavour in the first half, was rewarded only four minutes into the second half when referee, Glen Hart, spotted an infringement in the North Ferriby United box and pointed to the penalty spot. The resultant spot kick was coolly despatched by Karl Demidh. 1-1.

North Ferriby United were roused into action by the equaliser and within sixty seconds it was 2-1, another cross to Tom Denton's head and once again the net bulged after a powerful header from the big centre forward. Two minutes later, it was

3-1, with Denton turning provider, laying the ball off for Nathan Jarman to swivel and score with a neat finish.

During the week, the man who runs the Twitter site 'Non League Crowds' and also one of Alan's mates, Garry Marsden, had pledged to donate £1 to 'The Christie' every time a goal was scored from now on, on our FA Trophy journey, so Alan was rubbing his hands.

We suspected Mickleover Sports may be sapped of energy and morale by the third North Ferriby goal, but they continued to play stylish, attacking football and on the hour mark, a brilliant, powerfully struck shot from 25 yards from Anthony Griffith Junior made it 3-2.

Mickleover Sports had to press on in search of the equaliser but North Ferriby United are a hard side to break down with a resolute and well organised defence. They are also not a one-dimensional side who purely rely on the high ball to Denton, they can also play some neat football and four North Ferriby players were involved in a clever passage of play that led to the pacy Jason St Juste tapping in from inside the six yard box. 4-2 and there appeared little chance of a comeback this time, as North Ferriby had now taken the game by the scruff of the neck.

In the 84th minute, North Ferriby United turned defence to attack and a ball was played through for Tom Denton to run on to from the halfway line.

"He'll never score this," I said to Joel and Alan, "he's too slow."

"He might!" Alan replied.

My judgement was wrong. Denton is undeniably slow but I failed to factor a couple of things into my spontaneous assumption. Firstly, after scoring two headers,

Denton was on a hat-trick and he sensed this was his moment. Secondly, the Mickleover Sports team were weary and a little downtrodden and their full backs and centre backs did not chase back as determinedly as they might have done if it was still nil-nil.

A fifteen second period of football then played out in bizarre fashion. When I was a young child, the Six Million Dollar Man was my favourite programme and to emphasise his speed, action scenes were played out in slow motion. As Tom Denton closed in on goal, I was taken back to those slow motion moments, it was as though the world around him had stood still and only he was allowed to move. Denton carefully dribbled towards goal and as Chris Martin emerged from his goal line to narrow the angle, Denton prodded a low shot past him to complete his hat-trick and make it 5-2. North Ferriby United play in green and white, so as Denton celebrated, I immediately christened him the 'Jolly Green Giant', probably not the most original of names and I would guess he has been called this a thousand times before.

As neutrals watching a very entertaining, end to end game, as each team attacked, in the dying minutes, we willed them to score. In injury time, North Ferriby United substitute Ryan Kendall scrambled in a sixth to provide the final goal of an eight goal thriller and a further £16 in donations to Alan's 'Christie' pot. We had been through fourteen FA Cup rounds last season and never saw more than five goals in any one game so we were delighted to have seen eight, even Joel was pleased he had come along.

Alan and I were sad to say goodbye to Mickleover Sports, they are a great club and we hope they go on to have a terrific season, but we were also pleased to get a chance to watch North Ferriby United again. Each team that we had followed into a round had subsequently been knocked out in the next round :- Warrington, Mossley, New Mills and now Mickleover Sports had all perished at the next hurdle. We wondered whether our jinx would strike North Ferriby United in the First Round Proper.

Only four rounds in and already this route to Wembley had provided twenty two goals (although I had missed 5 at New Mills-Mossley). There were still six rounds to go and at least seven more games, as the semi-final is two legs, so on the way home we discussed whether our goal tally could surpass the 49 that we had witnessed in the FA Cup. We had now also gone sixteen rounds (12 in the FA Cup, 4 in the FA Trophy) without a replay. Other than a bit of fog at Mickleover it couldn't have worked out better!

FINAL SCORE :- North Ferriby United 6 Mickleover Sports 2

Monday 1st December 2014 – FA Trophy 1st Round Draw

The 1st Round Proper of the FA Trophy is when the Conference sides join in and a smaller club can potentially get the opportunity to pit their wits and footballing ability against a side who are aiming for League status come May. North Ferriby United are by no means minnows themselves and are only one League below the Conference, so are probably anticipating a decent run in the competition. Last season, North Ferriby reached the Quarter Final, before losing 2-1 at home to eventual runners up, Gosport Borough.

On Saturday, we were trying to establish whether the 1st Round Proper was still regionalised into Northern teams and Southern teams. Most supporters indicated the Regional divide finished after the Qualifying Rounds, so we waited for the draw with nervous anticipation as we thought we might have to travel as far afield as Dover or Torquay, not ideal when budgets are stretched anyway just before Christmas. We needn't have worried, as it transpires the Regional divide stays in place until the Third Round .

Just after midday, North Ferriby United tweeted that they had been drawn at home once more, this time against fellow Vanarama Conference North side, Boston United. A glance at the League table indicated they could barely be separated. This was going to be a tight one. Could it be 17th time unlucky for the dreaded replay?

Friday 5th December 2014

Ever since I wrote my first book, 'Forever Is Over', I have always been looking for ways to let people know about my books. Twitter has proved a more successful method than Facebook, as the whole thought process with Twitter is to interact with people who have common interests, rather than just interacting with friends. I enjoy the whole interaction side of Twitter, not just the self-publicising, and if you speak to my wife, she would probably tell you I have a Twitter addiction. This week, my Twitter addiction has provided an interesting opportunity as this afternoon, I was the 'Guest In The Comfy Chair' on Andy Comfort's show on BBC Radio Humberside.

On Tuesday, I received a Tweet from a lady called Lindsay, who is a researcher for the BBC, asking if I could follow her back on Twitter, so she could send me a direct message. Fellow Twitter addicts will know that only people you 'follow' are able to send you an exclusive 'direct message'. Intrigued, I followed Lindsay back and she was saying in her message to me that she was aware that I had written 'Another Saturday & Sweet F.A' about my journey through the FA Cup and would I like to be a guest on BBC Radio Humberside to talk about it?

I was excited about a new opportunity to talk about my book, live on air, but the logistics provided a difficulty. In October 2013, I started working as an Account Manager/Sales Rep for a Cheltenham based company called 'World of Warranty' and as I was now working Monday to Friday, nine to five, I could not just drive over to BBC Radio Humberside during the working day. Lindsay suggested I pop into a BBC studio near to where I was working, so I told her I would go to the BBC Radio Lancashire studio in Blackburn. I took a late lunch and nipped in there for just short of an hour.

I have previously been interviewed on Salford City radio, but that interview was recorded and edited, so I knew if I messed up, the recording could be paused and the question asked again. Being interviewed live by Andy Comfort for around half an hour, when I was in Blackburn, he was in Hull, we had never met and I had no real idea what he was going to ask me, provided an altogether more difficult challenge.

Thankfully, the interview turned out really well. Andy Comfort came across as a really likeable guy who had either done his research or it had been done for him by Lindsay as we chatted away about last year's FA Cup, the monologue I wrote for Johnny Vegas that was on BBC Radio Five Live, this year's FA Trophy, running five marathons and our fundraising efforts for 'The Christie'. I really enjoyed speaking to him and noticed there had been a spike in paperback sales of 'Another Saturday & Sweet FA' as a result of being on the show. One of the sports presenters at BBC Radio Lancashire came and had a chat with me subsequently and asked if I would also appear on one of their shows, early in the New Year, which I would be delighted to do if they want me.

Overall, since 'Another Saturday & Sweet FA' was released the week after the Arsenal victory in the FA Cup Final, sales have been steady rather than earth shatteringly good. I would say about 2000 have been bought in paperback or downloaded now, but 1200 of them were promotional ebook copies, given away free, so it is not 'Fever Pitch' as yet. In an age where there is so much reading material available free on-line though, to have 800 paid sales so far is encouraging. Perhaps if this FA Trophy book and next year's FA Vase somehow capture football fans imagination, some readers will return to where the adventure all started. I hope that is the case anyway.

Whilst mentioning where the adventure started, this year's FA Trophy adventure started for us at Warrington Town. On Sunday, they are away at Gateshead in the FA Cup 2nd Round. It is a midday kick off live on BT Sport. I will write an update as to how they got on. To be in the 3rd Round draw would be amazing for them, but Gateshead are an excellent side in the top half of the Conference so will be massive favourites to win. Having said that, I gave Warrington no chance against Exeter City in the 1st Round either.

Sunday 7th December 2014

Warrington Town's dream of a trip to a Premier League giant in the FA Cup 3rd Round is over. They lost 2-0 today at Gateshead. As mentioned on Friday, it was always going to be a big ask for Warrington. Defeating a Conference side at their own ground would have been a huge upset. Gateshead are in the fifth tier of English football and Warrington Town the eight tier, but Warrington acquitted themselves really well, on a difficult, windy day. The first goal came early, with an 8th minute finish in the six yard box from Matty Pattison, a South African former Newcastle United and Norwich City player. A Gateshead player that I am very familiar with from his days at Everton, former Welsh international, John Oster released Rob Ramshaw along the right wing, who went on a pacey run into the box before pulling a lovely ball back for Pattison to finish.

Warrington Town stuck to their task well, but, like in the previous round, they are part-timers playing against a professional opposition. Gateshead were dominating and Warrington Town's eight hundred strong band of supporters who had made the long journey up to the North East did not have too many chances to get excited about. They still made every effort to encourage their team on.

Warrington did manage a half chance when Lee Gaskell acrobatically sent an overhead kick wide. It was a spectacular effort and if it had found the back of the net, would have been the goal of the season.

The second half was more even than the first but chances were at a premium. Pattison could have had his and Gateshead's second on the hour mark when he sent the ball on to the post from a looping header. Metcalfe also sent a well struck 30 yard half volley just wide for Warrington. It took until the 90th minute for Gateshead to double their lead, goalkeeper Wills ran out of his box to collect a long ball from Gateshead with his feet, but he miscued his pass across to his centre back and it fell at the feet of Gateshead's substitute, Wright, who passed the ball into an unguarded net. 2-0 to Gateshead but Warrington can be very proud of their Cup exploits and their Chairman must be feeling on top of the world as two televised games have helped boost Warrington's revenues from the competition to an estimated £200 000. Warrington Town may have been hopeless in the FA Trophy but they have been fantastic in the FA Cup.

BOSTON UNITED

I would imagine someone has already written a book about the rise and fall of Boston United over the last twenty years, so I am not going to spend endless pages going into the most minute of details, but I do think an overview of what has happened to them in recent years is well worth telling. In some ways it is a similar story to that of Portsmouth and Leeds United, but in others it is even more shameful than what has happened to those two great clubs. Ambition initially led to success for Boston United that had not previously been experienced by those that ran the club or their fans. Ultimately though, success becomes a very difficult mistress to satisfy and when the almighty mess is untangled, it is the fans who are left after the party is over, that have to suffer the hangover. The fact that the success was achieved by dishonest means also adds to the unsavoury story.

Boston United were a non-League side from their formation in 1933 until 2002 when they were promoted to the Football League. During the first sixty nine years of their existence, they had some famous days. In 1955, they beat Derby County 6-1 in the FA Cup, which led to a tie against Tottenham Hotspur, which was attended by 46185 people, allegedly 10 000 of them Boston United fans. Sadly Boston lost 4-0.

Boston United are also former finalists of the FA Trophy. In 1985, they reached the final at the old Wembley stadium against Wealdstone. They lost 2-1 in front of a crowd of 20 775. I have noticed FA Trophy final crowds have held steady in the thirty years since and in recent years have occasionally been a lot higher, especially if former League clubs are involved in the Final. When Wrexham beat Grimsby Town in the 2013 Final, for example, there was a crowd of 35 266.

In 1998, Steve Evans, currently Rotherham United manager, took the helm at Boston United and the side were promoted from the Southern League to the Conference in 2000 and subsequently from the Conference to the Football League after winning the Conference in the 2001-02 season. Everything looked rosy as Boston United were finally in the Football League for the first time in their history, but the sweet taste of success soon turned sour.

In July 2002, the club hit the national sporting headlines for all the wrong reasons after the FA investigated them for contract irregularities, with players receiving far more money than their contracts, for tax purposes, disclosed. Pat Malkinson, the Chairman at the time, said Evans sorted out the player contracts personally and it transpired former League players like Mike Marsh and Ken Charlery amongst others, were paid a lot more than their contracts stipulated. Several years later, in 2006, Evans and Malkinson pleaded guilty in court for "conspiring to cheat the public revenue" and were each given suspended sentences, but prior to that the FA handed out its own football related punishments.

Prior to the start of the 2002-03 League season, the FA decided to dock Boston United four points for the upcoming season, as well as fine them £100 000 for the contract irregularities. This incensed officials at Dagenham & Redbridge who felt they were the main victims of Boston United's indiscretions. Dagenham & Redbridge had only missed out on promotion to the Football League on goal difference and felt the points deduction should have been deducted from the previous season's points tally which would have handed the Champions spot and a place in the League to Dagenham & Redbridge. A track & field analogy would be Ben Johnson being allowed to keep his Olympic Gold from Seoul 1988, but being banned from future races. It doesn't make sense. Following on from the points deduction, in January 2003, Steve Evans was suspended from the game for twenty months.

It must have been a very strange period for Boston United fans. Having had the euphoric feelings of promotion taken from you so quickly by the discovery of financial indiscretions by your club's officials must have been very difficult to take. Many supporters who supported the club through many years of mediocrity felt that they had had their moment of pride stolen from them. Several washed their hands of the club altogether and began watching neighbouring Boston Town. The level of discontent amongst fans rose once more when Steve Evans returned as Manager in March 2004.

This whole period of Boston United's history is fascinating, if not always pretty and as stated previously, I am loathe to concentrate too much of this book on it. The years that followed in their short period in the Football League contained their fair share of dramatic moments, culminating in a game against Wrexham in May 2007. Going into the last game of the season, Macclesfield, Boston United and Wrexham all faced potential relegation to the Conference and it transpired that Macclesfield were to get the point they needed against Notts County so the defeated team in the Wrexham-Boston United encounter would drop out the League.

Boston United actually took the lead but a second half comeback saw Wrexham coming out winners 3-1. Prior to the game, Boston had been teetering on the brink of administration. Facing a ten point deduction as punishment, in the season they entered administration, Boston United Chairman, Jim Rodwell immediately put the club into administration when Wrexham took a 2-1 lead in the 87th minute. This was an obvious attempt to ensure the points deduction took place in the 2006-07 season, rather than the following one. A further Wrexham goal condemned them to a 3-1 defeat and a return to non-League football.

Boston had managed to avoid a points deduction in the season they were promoted from the Conference in 2002, but they weren't going to be as lucky as they dropped back out the League. Staff and players at Boston United had not been paid for the last two months of the season, as the club had crippling debts and once they entered a CVA (Company Voluntary Arrangement) meaning they could not repay 100% of their footballing debts, FA rules dictated that they must be demoted two Leagues rather than one. Boston United started the following season in the Blue Square North (Conference North). Two years later, they dropped to the third tier of Non-League football, the Unibond Premier, and only avoided a further drop the following season, with a last game of the season 1-0 victory over Cammell Laird.

Subsequently, having had a tumultuous period in their history, things have steadied and slowly improved. In the 2009-10 season, Boston United were promoted back to the Blue Square North via the play offs, under the management team of former Ilkeston Town bosses, Rob Scott and Paul Hurst. The following season, the club finished third in the Blue Square North, only losing out in their promotion push in the play offs, losing on penalties to Guiseley. During the season, they had lost the management pair of Scott and Hurst to Grimsby Town. A few managers have been and gone since, including former Nottingham Forest striker, Jason Lee, but in March 2013, Dennis Greene took the helm. Last season, 2013-14 was his first full season and he guided the club to sixth position, narrowly missing out on the Top Five finish they needed to be in the Play Offs. This season, the Play Offs seem to be the aim again, as Boston United are in a top half position in the Conference North and so far, are unbeaten in November and December. As mentioned when the draw was made, on paper, the tie with North Ferriby United seems like it will be a very even clash. If I was to hazard a guess who would win, on current form, I would have to say Boston United.

Saturday 13th December 2014 – FA Trophy 1st Round

North Ferriby United v Boston United

Attendance – 321

One of the things I have loved about last year's FA Cup journey and this year's FA Trophy one, is that from time to time uncanny things happen. By this, I don't mean one in a million events, just happy co-incidences. Drawing Everton in last year's FA Cup being one and this year twice getting to go to North Ferriby, three miles from the house of one of my closest friends, Jamie Lowe. For this game though, an even bigger co-incidence has come about.

Gordon Johnson, a friend of mine who was a former referee and an Assistant Referee up to Championship level, has taken a particular interest in our FA Cup and FA Trophy journeys. Once 'Another Saturday & Sweet FA' came out, he has met up with me a couple of times to take several copies off me and has regularly publicised it to his friends. As we have gone through the FA Trophy journey, he has been following our progress with interest and is keen to come along to a game if opportunity allows. These days, Gordon is the 'Referee Development Co-Ordinator' at Liverpool County FA and contacted me on Facebook to say he knows the referee for the North Ferriby United against Boston United tie. He explained it is the son of a former Premier League ref and this ref is himself already swiftly moving up the ranks and is a Premier League Assistant Referee already.

As soon as Gordon mentioned the Premier League Assistant Referee status, I started to wonder about who it was. My two sons, Brad and Joel, go to Parklands High School in Chorley and are always coming back from school with stories about their PE teacher, Mr Salisbury running the line in a Premier League game. Whilst sending messages back and forth to Gordon, I couldn't remember the teacher's name, but I quickly established that Michael Salisbury, the ref Gordon knew, was a PE teacher in the Preston or Chorley area, so was 99% sure it would be Brad and Joel's teacher. A quick check with the lads confirmed their teacher was Michael Salisbury. Our next game was going to be refereed by the lads PE teacher!

Brad and Joel like Mr Salisbury. They are both into their football, so to have a teacher who has a Premier League connection cannot fail to impress them, but they say he is a teacher who is fairly strict but one that everyone respects. Both of them initially said they would like to come to the game. Brad only half-jokingly said he could go to the game and hurl abuse at the ref and there wouldn't be a thing he could do about it! I explained he may not be able to do anything during the game but I'm sure he would subsequently find some way of getting you back at school. Brad wants to stand for School Sports Captain next year, when he starts his final year at the school, so wouldn't dare to blot his copybook with one of his PE teachers.

Prior to the game both boys found better things to do with their Saturday than come to North Ferriby, so backed out of coming along. On a more positive front, Jamie Lowe said he would love to come along to this one, having missed the previous round. We again arranged to call at his house, have lunch and then go to the game from there. As usual, I picked Alan up from Buckshaw Parkway train station and we headed East to North Ferriby. We had sandwiches and hot sausage rolls at Jamie's in Brough then headed to the game.

On arriving at the Eon Visual Media Stadium, we started to do our usual lap of the ground, but as we passed the players and officials entrance to the pitch from the changing rooms, who should we pass but Michael Salisbury. He was just heading out with his Assistants to do his warm up on the pitch and I almost bumped into him.

"Excuse me, Michael, I'm Calvin Wade, Brad and Joel Wade's Dad," I explained, shaking his hand.

Michael Salisbury, a young ref in his late twenties broke out into a broad smile.

"Do you know what? Joel said to me in school that his Dad was going to a game that I was reffing at, on Saturday and I said he'd made a mistake. I told him I wasn't running the line in the League this weekend, I was reffing miles away. I can't believe you are here!"

Anyway, we had a brief chat and I then let him go on his way and we continued on our way around the ground.

"If I didn't know you better," Jamie laughed, "I would say that was staged and you asked the ref to walk out the moment you went past."

Jamie and Alan are both friendly characters and immediately developed a bit of a rapport, to an extent at my expense. After a lap of the ground, we went into the club bar and I bought a couple of pints of Guinness for Jamie and me, and a soft drink for Alan. Whilst chatting over a pint, Alan told Jamie about the fact I had missed the New Mills v Mossley game.

"That's it," Jamie said in mock indignation, "I've been conned. I thought you two were doing every round of the FA Trophy, but it appears one of you is an imposter. There's no way I'm buying that bloody book now. In fact, having been today, I might write one myself."

It was great having Jamie with us, as it adds to the dynamic. With my Dad and Phil Cooper not being a part of the journey this year (or in Phil's case just a cameo role for the first game), Alan and I are spending a lot of time travelling round as a footballing pair, so to have someone else to share jokes with, and enjoy a bit of banter with, certainly freshens things up. Jamie is always good fun to be around and is very interested in hearing other people's stories, so was fascinated by Alan's groundhopping adventures. Another co-incidence came to light too, when Jamie revealed that as a 14 year old lad from Skegness, Lincolnshire, he actually went to the 1985 FA Trophy Final at Wembley to support Boston when they lost to Wealdstone.

Once this game kicked off, we pointed out Tom Denton to Jamie, who already had a Duncan Ferguson like cult status for Alan and me. He had terrorised the Mickleover Sports centre backs, but after a few minutes, it became obvious that the Boston United centre back who had been designated the role of marking Denton, a lad called Carl Piergianni, was an excellent player and was not going to give Denton an easy time. In fact, over the ninety minutes, Piergianni won that personal duel hands down. Piergianni is a former Peterborough United schoolboy and joined Boston United from Stockport County. He looks like a lad who could play at Conference or lower League level quite easily.

The game, played on a bitter winter's day, took a while to warm up. Boston were the better passing side, but wanted to show North Ferriby that they were up for the physical side of the game too. Both sides were putting it about a bit and a few late tackles were flying in. Michael Salisbury, the ref, appeared to have control and has an unflappable style but I mentioned to Alan and Jamie, that maybe if he had showed a yellow or two, early on, it would have taken the niggle out of the game. We weren't sure if there is any history between the teams, but they didn't appear to be the closest of friends.

Boston had brought about 100 travelling fans and we started to chat to one or two of those around us. Every time North Ferriby's right back, Jamie Yates, was on the ball, he was getting abuse off them, so we asked what the reason was. It transpires that Yates is a former Boston player. He had played over thirty times for Rotherham United before joining Boston and enjoyed two successful seasons in 2009-10 and 2010-11, but apparently having spoken at a Boston United supporters club meeting about his love for the club, he left days later for a better deal at Gainsborough Trinity.

The first half had very few chances for either team and neither goalkeeper was tested. Liam King had a shot that was deflected off a Boston defender and struck the post, but other than that, it was the tight encounter we had been expecting. When the ref blew the half-time whistle, to end a scoreless first half, we gratefully went in search of coffees and Jamie asked if he could go home now as he couldn't feel his toes.

At half-time, once he had been warmed up by his hot drink, Jamie was asking about the FA Cup journey we had been on the previous season. Alan explained that in a lot of games there had been a turning point that had swung the game in one teams favour, for example Guisborough hitting the bar when 1-0 up against Workington. At 2-0 they may have gone on to win, but a 1-0 lead was always vulnerable against a team several Leagues higher and Workington went on to win the game 4-1.

Boston, who we thought had edged the first half, came out strongly in the second half, pushing North Ferriby back and for the first time in the game, started to create chances. A corner was taken by Notts County loanee, Greg Tempest and the ball fell to Marc Newsham, a dangerous centre forward who has bagged over 100 goals for Boston since he signed in 2009, who looked for all the world to have broken the deadlock with a low shot, but it hit the post and rebounded to safety.

After surviving the strong passage of play from Boston early in the second half, North Ferriby began to get back in to the game and Jamie Yates, who continued to get abuse with every touch, almost silenced his detractors when he struck a 20 yard dipping free kick that left Joel Dixon, the Sunderland loanee keeper stranded, but cannoned off the bar. The game was really end to end now and was a far better spectacle than the first half.

On 67 minutes, the deadlock was finally broken. In nineteen previous FA Cup and FA Trophy games this season and last, we had yet to see a game with less than two goals, so Alan and I were blaming Jamie for potentially providing our first goalless draw. This was avoided though when Jamie Yates lost possession to Mark Jones, who whipped in a dangerous cross that was met by the head of Marc Newsham, who accurately guided the ball back across the goal and into the back of the net. 1-0 to Boston.

As the Boston United players celebrated delightedly in front of us, Alan pointed out that we were a jinx for every team in this competition. Each team we had followed into the round, had lost their next game. This had happened to Warrington, Mossley, New Mills, Mickleover Sports and now looked like it was happening to North Ferriby United.

North Ferriby United are a gutsy team though and one thing was for certain, they would not go down without a fight. As is always the case, when a team has to begin to throw caution to the wind, they can leave spaces for the opposition forwards to exploit. The front three of Kaine Felix, Mark Jones and Marc Newsham are all quick for Boston United, especially Kaine Felix and from a North Ferriby United attack that broke down, Boston released Mark Jones who cut through the Ferriby defence, only to be brought down by North Ferriby's Danny Hone, inside the box. As Hone was the last man, ref Michael Salisbury had no choice but to show a red card to the defender. North Ferriby not only faced a penalty which, if converted, would take the score to 2-0, but also had to play the remainder of the game with ten men. The odds looked stacked against them.

At this stage, it would be wise to cast your mind back to Alan's pivotal moments that changed games we had seen. The penalty taker for Boston United was Scott Garner, a vastly experienced defender that has captained England's C team, which is the non-League national side. Having started his career at Leicester City, Garner has gone on to play for Mansfield Town, Grimsby Town and Cambridge United, as well as Boston. In goal for North Ferriby United, was Adam Nicklin, who had impressed me in the two games I had seen him, by being a dependable, if unspectacular keeper. As a former keeper myself, 'unspectacular' is not a bad thing. I would rather the goalkeeper of my team caught a ball than dramatically pushed it over the bar.

Adam Nicklin does not have anywhere near as impressive a footballing C.V as Scott Garner. He was playing Sunday League football for West Ella and was all set to a move to Hall Road Rangers, when his manager at West Ella arranged for Nicklin to go for a trial at Frickley. Frickley were managed by Billy Heath, at the time and he was impressed by Nicklin, so much so, when Billy Heath moved on to become manager at North Ferriby United, he signed Adam Nicklin once more. From what I have seen so far, that was sound judgement.

Scott Garner struck his penalty firmly towards Adam Nicklin's top left corner, but Nicklin spread himself well and managed to get a powerful palm under the ball and pushed it on to the bar. It was a superb save. The ball was cleared by the North Ferriby defence and Boston had missed a golden opportunity to guarantee a place in the Second Round.

"It would have been all over if that had have gone in," Alan observed.

"It's not now though," Jamie said, "wouldn't it be funny if North Ferriby United equalised and you two had to go to Boston for the replay in midweek?"

"No," Alan and I said in unison.

"No, it wouldn't be funny, it would be hilarious," Jamie laughed, "I'm off to Center Parcs this week, so I couldn't come, but I'd think of the pair of you freezing your nuts off in Boston on a cold winter's night."

"North Ferriby won't score," I said, trying to convince myself as I watched them surge forward in waves.

If I am honest, I thought there would be another goal, but I expected the ten men of North Ferriby to tire and be caught on the break. Dennis Greene, the Boston United manager, was settling for 1-0 though and he took off goalscorer, Newsham, in the 83rd minute and replaced him with midfielder, Jamie McGhee. North Ferriby continued to press forward though and their spirited display was rewarded in the 89th minute. Liam King, an attacking midfielder, put a ball in to Ryan Kendall, a substitute who had only recently rejoined the club after a brief spell at Harrogate Town. His Wikipedia page states he is 6 feet 1 inches tall, which means he was either standing on a milk crate or his toes when measured or he quite simply lied. What Kendall lacks in height, however, he more than makes up for in goalscoring ability. He scored 46 goals in his first 75 game spell at North Ferriby and when the ball fell to him, with his back to goal, he turned neatly and fired an unstoppable shot past Joel Dixon into the corner of the net. A last minute equaliser. 1-1.

"That is absolutely hilarious!" Jamie stated in between hysterics.

"It's a f####n' nightmare, it's about a 300 mile round trip to Boston," Alan groaned.

One minute later it was all over. It was announced the replay was to be played on Tuesday 16th December at 7:45 p.m.

We headed for the exit and as we walked along the path to the road, which was parallel to the allotments that back on to North Ferriby's ground, I began to panic. Jamie was complaining about frostbite as it was still bitterly cold, Alan was complaining about a trip to Boston the week before Christmas and it suddenly dawned on me, Alan could be in trouble maintaining his 100% record of going to every FA Cup & Trophy game.

"Alan, we might be struggling here," I explained.

"Why, Cal?"

"Alison is on nights this week and I don't trust the lads enough to leave them on their own for more than a couple of hours. I might have to miss Tuesday night."

"No problem, mate."

"Alan, it is a problem. How the hell are you going to get from Failsworth to Boston and back on a Tuesday night? There won't be any direct trains going from Boston to Manchester at that time of night and it's not as though you can jump on the team bus like you did at Mickleover Sports v New Mills."

As previously explained Alan can't drive. All his footballing travels are done by coach, tram and train, with the occasional car journey as a passenger.

"Don't you worry about me, Cal, I'll get there mate. Even if I have to bed down somewhere for the night, like on a bench in a train station, I'll get there."

I also had another thought and maybe I was thinking about it so hard, Jamie could read my mind.

"Calvin, if you miss another game, that book of yours is only going to be about ten pages long! Remind me to give it a miss."

Jamie was only winding me up in jovial fashion, but he had a point. Having missed the New Mills-Mossley game, I didn't know whether I could justify writing a book about our FA Trophy adventures if I was to miss another game.

"Alan, if I do miss another one, you are going to have to get a writing pad out mate and this book is going to be written by Calvin Wade and Alan Oliver."

"Don't worry Cal, it'll be right."

I wasn't convinced. I realised I needed to get to the game. I needed to find the lads a babysitter.

FINAL SCORE :- North Ferriby United 1 Boston United 1

Sunday 14th December 2014

With things being tight financially in recent years, mine and Alison's social life has not stopped, but the locations have certainly changed. Rather than going for meals out, we tend to go to friends or invite friends to ours, so as a consequence we do not have a regular babysitter that I can call on. With Brad being fourteen now, the boys can be left for a few hours, I just don't trust them enough to leave them from late afternoon until after midnight. If they didn't argue, fight and wind each other up, it would be a different matter, but I don't like the idea of returning to a trashed house and broken bones.

In my head, today, I have run through the children of friends in the road who are old enough to take on babysitting and peacekeeping duties. Grace is at Manchester Metropolitan University, Hannah has moved in with her boyfriend, works full-time and is beyond the age where a few extra quid from babysitting is an attractive proposition. Joe up the road has gone to University, but hang on, his brother Jake is in Sixth Form, he might do it.

I called round at Jake's Mum and Dad's, Geoff and Kay's, and as Jake wasn't in, tried to explain the whole footballing story to a bewildered Geoff. He probably lost interest half way through as I droned on, as he suddenly perked up when I mentioned Boston.

"Boston, Massachusetts?"

"No, Boston, Lincolnshire."

"I was going to say. I'll ask him when he gets in, Calvin, but I can't see it being a problem."

Geoff knocked around at ours about half an hour later to say he had spoken to Jake and it was fine, he could babysit. Brad then became aware of my plot. After Geoff left, Brad went into a rant about how embarrassing it was that I was paying for a babysitter for him when he was almost fifteen years old. It was humiliating, I was told. He would be staying the night somewhere else rather than have to suffer the shame of having a 17 year old come around to look after him.

"Act like a 15 year old and I will treat you like a 15 year old," I explained.

"You've had some stupid ideas in your time, Dad, but this is the most stupid one ever," Brad moaned.

I wasn't concerned. If every decision I ever made, satisfied Brad and Joel, I would be failing as a parent and raising two pampered, unappreciative kids. Not that they appreciate me now, but maybe when they get older they might. As I keep telling them, my job isn't to make them like me, my job is to make them into decent human beings. I sound like a tyrant saying that, which I'm not, if you ask my Mum and Dad, they would say I'm a soft touch. Anyway, that's the babysitter sorted. I said to Geoff for Jake to come around about seven, just before Alison goes in on nights.

I phoned Alan to let him know that he would not be journeying to Boston alone and he sounded a relieved man. He had been looking at train timetables and he would have had to change trains three times on his way home and would have arrived back at Manchester at quarter to five in the morning! He said he would have just gone straight into work from there. With luck on our side, we should be back now at about midnight.

With the uncertainty over, I can now look forward to a trip to Boston on Tuesday night. It may not be our only trip there either, Boston United looked a decent side and I can see them causing a few teams problems. I wouldn't imagine Jamie will be returning to Wembley with them, thirty years on, but a run through to the Quarters, like North Ferriby did last year, is certainly a possibility.

Monday 15th December 2014

I work at home on a Monday, booking appointments for the rest of the week and doing some administrative work. This fits in nicely with the FA Trophy draw, as it always takes place at midday on a Monday. There is obviously more of a gap this time around as Christmas is coming, so the 2nd Round games won't take place until Saturday 10th January.

The FA Trophy draw is very different to the FA Cup draw, because it attracts very little interest from anyone other than the fans of the clubs still in it. TalkSport radio station have taken to hosting a Qualifying Round draw for the FA Cup, which is great because there is not as much interest as there should be in the Non-League stages of the FA Cup, but the FA Trophy draw passes without any drama at all. No celebrities are asked to draw the balls, it is just drawn by the 'Football Association' officials and then the clubs are emailed with details of the draw. In this age of social media, tweets regarding the draw are normally posted by about five past twelve.

Today, Boston United or North Ferriby United have been drawn at home to Hyde F.C, another team in the Conference North. Hyde are struggling though and they are rooted at the bottom of the League, having only won two League games all season. Interestingly, one of those two wins was a 1-0 home win against North Ferriby United.

As the draw is still regionalised, a home draw for Boston United is about as far afield as we could travel. I don't mind that though. This is a small island and any team can be reached on a Saturday afternoon from an early morning start. The slight concern, once the North-South divide is dispensed with in the next round, is that we end up having a Tuesday night replay in Kent or Devon.

Both Boston and North Ferriby must be looking at the draw and thinking it is a real opportunity to get through to the last sixteen. Hyde are struggling for a reason and a home draw against them may not draw the biggest of crowds, but a victory would put another few thousand pounds in the kitty. Once you get to the last sixteen, Wembley no longer seems like a distant dream.

We are all set for tomorrow night. I am going to see a load of car dealers on the East side of Manchester tomorrow and will then be going straight from there to pick Alan up. I have warned Jake, the babysitter, that I will be back at around half past midnight and even later if there is extra time. There is no second replay, if the game isn't decided tomorrow in ninety minutes, there is extra time and then penalties. I am sure it will be another tight encounter, so extra time would be no great surprise.

Tuesday 16th December 2014 – FA Trophy 1st Round Replay

Boston United v North Ferriby United

Attendance – 671

Well, it was always going to happen eventually. Our 19th round of FA football in the FA Cup and FA Trophy over this season and last, has finally delivered a replay. Similarly to the Mickleover – New Mills rematch, the logistics of getting to the game were the headache. Once that was sorted, a trip to Boston is all part of the adventure and all day I wanted work to finish and the journey to Boston to begin.

I phoned Alan after my last call to a car dealer's, when I was two minutes from his house and he was still on his way home from work, but said his daughter, Jordan, would let me in and make me a cup of coffee. I had met Jordan many times before during our FA Cup exploits, as she had been to many of the games with her Dad, so it was good to see her again. She was gearing up for a night out in Manchester for a pub quiz, but sat down for ten minutes and had a chat with me. Jordan told me her Dad wasn't at all well as he had a really heavy cold and also severe toothache.

"You know what he's like though, Calvin. There was no way he was going to miss a game."

Alan arrived home a few minutes later looking flustered, under the weather but still raring to go. Perhaps laughter isn't the best medicine after all, maybe it's football.

We said our goodbyes to Jordan and we were soon on our way. It was a cold, damp, winter's night with some heavy rain forecast heading West from Ireland and throwing a blanket of black cloud over much of the North of England. Thankfully for us, it was only due to hit Boston at around 10 p.m. As it was not bitterly cold and several degrees above freezing, we decided to head over the Snake Pass, the route from East Manchester to Sheffield through the Peak District. A scenic run on a bright summer's day, but just the most direct route on a dark winter's evening. The road (A57) is often shut on cold winter's nights as it becomes treacherous when icy, but the forecast rain was likely to keep the temperatures up and icy conditions at bay.

Boston is not the easiest place to get to. It is a few miles from the East coast, forty miles directly East from Nottingham, but of the 117 miles from Failsworth to Boston, only twenty one were on Motorways, the rest were 'A' roads. As we were leaving during peak times, there was also a slight concern that we could miss kick off, if we hit too much traffic on the way, but thankfully we arrived in Boston by seven o'clock.

Boston United's ground is currently sponsored and rather than having its historical name of York Street, it is called 'The Jakemans Stadium'. Jakemans are a menthol confectioners from Boston. I know them only too well, as Alison swears by their throat and chest sweets every time she has a heavy cold and I often get sent down to the supermarket during the winter to pick up a packet.

As we were relatively early, we were able to park in the residential street just outside the ground. The stadium still has the old style prominent floodlights beaming out light from the four corners of the ground. Thirty years ago, most grounds were spotted by the floodlight pylons first and there is a warming, old fashioned feel to any club that have retained them. Unfortunately, the reasons for Boston United's retention of their old floodlights are probably economically related. They probably could not afford to buy new ones and also as it is their intention to move to a new stadium, it does not make sense to part with a large sum of money for lights that will only be needed until the new stadium is built.

One thing I realised on the way to the game, was that Alan was keen for a North Ferriby United win. Tonight's game marks our third game to see them, equalling the record of Burscough, Workington, Stevenage, Everton and Arsenal, last season, and New Mills and Mickleover Sports this, as our most watched team in the FA Cup and FA Trophy. We have always tried to retain our neutrality but the more you see a team, the more your allegiance shifts. When Mickleover Sports played North Ferriby, we probably favoured a Mickleover win, now it's North Ferriby's turn for our support. From a personal perspective, it is always good to catch up with Jamie too and a North Ferriby win would ensure we would be calling back in on him, in January.

We bought a programme each outside the ground and Alan asked the programme seller if the game would be segregated and there would be a home and away end. The gentleman was unsure, but he said there was definitely an away turnstile and pointed us in the direction we needed to go, past the club shop. When we got there, the man on the turnstile told us we were the first North Ferriby United fans to arrive. Later, when the attendance of 671 was confirmed, we were told this included ten away fans. We had added 25% on to the away support.

Once we were inside 'The Jakeman Stadium', the old fashion feel to the place did not diminish. Running along one side of the pitch is a large seated area, but the other three sides are largely terraced, with one massive terraced area behind the far goal, which was a smaller version of Liverpool and Sheffield Wednesday's Spion Kop's of yesteryear. The inquisitive side of me once wondered where the term 'Spion

Kop' came from and a quick internet check revealed (via Wikipedia) that their steep banks of terracing resembled a hill near Ladysmith, South Africa that was the scene of the 'Battle of Spion Kop' in January 1900, during the Boer War.

Alan and I took our usual corner flag photographs and realised although there was an away turnstile, there was no segregation. I think Alan liked the idea of staying in the allocated section for away fans, probably because at that stage in proceedings, we were the away fans, but given a choice I always prefer to watch a game from the halfway line rather than from behind a goal, so I suggested we move into the Boston section. As we were walking around, a bearded Bostonian gentleman in his forties, who we had met at North Ferriby, came over to shake us by the hand and said he had followed us on Twitter. He was a warm friendly guy and was hopeful of a Boston victory. It seemed wise not to mention that we hoped they lost.

At quarter to eight, the game was under way and the skies over Boston were clear, which made me particularly glad that I had invested in a new pair of winter gloves and a deerstalker type hat that covered my ears, as it was bitterly cold.

North Ferriby United full back, Jamie Yates, may have thought he had taken some abuse from the Boston fans at North Ferriby on Saturday, but it was nothing compared to the abuse he received in the first forty five minutes. Terrace chants have been a rare thing on the FA Trophy trail, but Boston have enough of a following for a good old singalong and tonight's sing-alongs were often questioning Jamie Yates parentage and the fact that Boston United fans felt they knew what Jamie Yates was and it wasn't anything particularly pleasant. Just before half time, Yates pulled up after a fairly innocuous challenge and did not reappear for the second half.

Whether he was genuinely injured or just thought he had endured enough abuse for one evening, perhaps we will never know.

The first half was a bit of a tame affair, but disappointingly Boston did not seem to be playing with the same flair that we had witnessed on Saturday at North Ferriby. Both goalkeepers, North Ferriby's Adam Nicklin and Boston's young Sunderland loanee, Joel Dixon, both impressed and it appeared to be one of those nights that required a catastrophic mistake or a moment of sheer brilliance to break the deadlock.

North Ferriby's best chance in the first half came from a great cross from the much maligned Jamie Yates. He whipped in an inviting ball from wide on the right that only required the slightest of touches to end up in the back of the Boston United net. Adam Bolder came closest to getting on the end of it, but just failed to make contact.

Boston had a number of half chances but their best chance of all was self-made by Greg Tempest. He struck a sweet volley from twenty yards out that dipped and curled as it moved towards goal, but was well watched by Ferriby keeper Nicklin, who managed to parry it away from danger. 0-0 seemed about right at the break and as Alan and I headed over to get a warming hot drink, we began to question if this game was destined for penalties.

Boston's pitch is big and wide and with them being a better passing side than the tougher, more hard working, resilient North Ferriby side, we had expected Boston to begin to dominate proceedings as the North Ferriby side tired but that is not how things transpired. North Ferriby remind me and Alan of the mid-90s Everton side that Joe Royle managed, fit, hard working and with a 'Dogs of War' spirit. The

Everton side that won the FA Cup in 1995 had a tricky winger, Anders Limpar who was capable of moments of genius. North Ferriby don't quite have a Limpar, but in Jason St Juste they have someone who has dribbling skills and pace. On a large pitch, he is a great outlet when under pressure. He went on one mazy run that beat three Boston defenders and pulled the ball back only for Boston to scramble clear. This was a signal of intent from St Juste but Boston did not heed the warning. A few minutes later, in the 72nd minute, a weak back pass from Boston's Liam Marrs was latched on to by Jason St Juste, he rounded Joel Dixon in the Boston goal and slid the ball into the empty net. 1-0 to North Ferriby.

Alan and I are astute enough to know that when you have 669 people around you, only eight of which are North Ferriby fans, it would be lunacy to celebrate wildly, but we exchanged a contented smile. Rather than try to get back into the game by passing North Ferriby off the park, Boston bizarrely opted to go more 'Route One' which just played into North Ferriby's hands. Boston forced several throw ins deep into the North Ferriby half and rather than take a short throw and whip a quick ball in to the likes of Newsham, to allow him to utilise his predatory skills, they threw the ball long. North Ferriby countered this by bringing 6 feet 5 inch man mountain, Tom Denton, back for every throw and time after time the ball landed in the ideal spot for him to head clear. Still Boston refused to change their tactics. It was frustrating for Alan and me to watch, but it must have been painful for the Boston supporters.

The refusal by Boston to adopt a different plan was further punished in injury time. North Ferriby counter attacked and Ryan Kendall, who along with Adam Nicklin had done most to force a replay by scoring in Saturday's game, had a shot that was well saved by Joel Dixon, but he was first to the rebound and gleefully tapped home. 2-0 to North Ferriby United.

Hundreds of Boston fans immediately headed for the exit and Alan and I followed them out. We don't like leaving before the final whistle though, so stopped at the corner flag by the exit, to watch the resultant kick off and moments later, the final whistle blew. Boston had been the better side on Saturday, but this time around, North Ferriby United were worthy winners.

Our long journey home was made longer by part of the Snake Pass being shut and us having to follow a diversion. I still managed to drop Alan off by midnight and was home by quarter to one, to allow Jake the babysitter to get home to bed. Despite Brad complaining about the need for Jake to come, he had actually proved useful, as he had helped Brad with his German homework.

So, North Ferriby United are through to the last 32 and with a home tie against Hyde to come, they must fancy their chances of a last 16 place. Having lost to Gosport Borough in last year's Quarter Final, they only have to go two rounds better to be walking out at Wembley. There will be better teams in the competition but perhaps not many with more spirit. I certainly don't think they will fear anyone. One or two teams may fear them though.

FINAL SCORE :- Boston United 0 North Ferriby United 2

Wednesday 17th December 2014

One thing that winds me up in sport, is people who don't know how to either win or lose with dignity. If you win, celebrate your victory, but empathise with the defeated party. If you lose, look at how you lost and even if you felt you were the better side or luck was against you, appreciate the merits of the victors.

I am saying this today, because I have been really disappointed to read the comments from Boston United manager, Dennis Greene, following their defeat last night. If anything, they say more about him as a man, than they do about the North Ferriby United side that he has taken a swipe at. Greene has commented, that North Ferriby are "horrible to watch", that they have a direct approach that centres around Tom Denton and that they feign injury, dive and buy free kicks.

My opinion on North Ferriby United (and Alan's for that matter and we don't agree on everything) is that they are a hardworking side who play to their strengths. When keeper Nicklin takes goal kicks, he aims for Denton, but it's a percentage game. If I was a keeper and I had a 6 feet 5 inch striker, I would be aiming for him too, on the basis that he is going to win a higher percentage of aerial balls than Ryan Kendall or Jason St Juste. Are they direct the rest of the time? No. Did their goals at Boston stem more from tricky winger St Juste than Denton? Yes. Did they feign injury, dive and buy free kicks any more than Boston United? Absolutely not. Both teams did it in equal proportion. I agree it is an unpleasant aspect of football in general, but get your own house in order before you start throwing stones.

Having only seen Boston United twice, it is hard to know what to make of them, but I suspect they are more like the team we saw on Saturday and will end up finishing in or around the play off spots in Conference North. Do I think they will finish higher than North Ferriby? Probably. Do they have North Ferriby's backbone? Not from the evidence of last night.

I wish Boston United well. The fans that have stuck with them deserve some further success in this bounce back period, but their manager needs to shoulder some responsibility for their failure. For starters, he should have put a stop to the hurling of throw-ins on to the head of Tom Denton. Earlier tonight, I sent him a series of tweets spelling this out and saying having seen North Ferriby United three times, I have only seen one bad tackle, Matt Wilson's against Mickleover. In the two games against Boston United, there wasn't one. I am a neutral, if I had witnessed a succession of tackles like Matt Wilson's, I would want to see Ferriby knocked out this competition, but it hasn't happened. A reply from Dennis Greene hasn't been forthcoming either. I hope he regrets what he says and it would be nice if he had the good grace to apologise to North Ferriby United for his ill advised words, otherwise it just sounds like he has spent the last 24 hours munching on a bunch of sour grapes.

Thursday 18th December 2014

With no further FA Trophy games now until the second week in January, I guess now is a good time to catch up on which teams are left in the competition.

First Round Proper – Saturday 13th December

Northern Section

Nuneaton 0 Grimsby Town 2

Hyde 4 Spennymoor Town 2

Altrincham 1 Macclesfield 0

AFC Fylde 3 Gainsborough T 0

Guiseley 0 Chorley 2

Lincoln City 0 Alfreton 2

North Ferriby United 1 Boston United 1

Gateshead 2 Halesowen 0

Southport 1 Wrexham 1

Ramsbottom Utd 0 Stockport County 3

AFC Telford Utd 1 Chester 1

FC United 4 Harrogate Town 0

Worcester City P Halifax Town P

Bradford Park Av. P Kidderminster H. P

Southern Section

Aldershot Town 0 Burgess Hill Town 1

Weymouth 1 Havant & W. 1

Bishop's Stortford 0 Torquay United 5

Lowestoft Town 1 Dover Athletic 3

Ebbsfleet United 1 Welling United 1

Wealdstone 1 Hayes & Yeading 0

Wimborne Town 0 Oxford City 3

Weston Super Mare 1 Farnborough 3

Dartford 2 Solihull Moors 0

Woking 2 Eastleigh 0

Hemel Hempstead 1 Sutton United 0

Basingstoke Town 2 Gosport Borough 2

Bromley 2 Leiston 0

Forest Green 2 Didcot Town 2

Bristol Rovers 0 Bath City 2

Maidenhead Utd 2 Poole Town 1

Braintree Town 1 AFC Sudbury 0

Concord Rangers 0 Barnet 0

One of the things that struck me about these results was that goals were at a premium. Six of the thirty games only had one goal or were goalless. This shows how lucky Alan and I have been on our FA Cup & Trophy trails. In our twenty one games (including the abandoned game at Mickleover Sports), we have yet to see a game with less than two goals and have seen an amazing 75 goals in 21 games (and there probably would have been more in the first Mickleover Sports v New Mills game if it hadn't been abandoned).

Since Saturday, a few of the replays and postponed games have now taken place and the results were as follows :-

Monday 15th December

Bradford Park Avenue 1 Kidderminster Harriers 4

Tuesday 16th December

Boston United 0 North Ferriby United 2

Wrexham 2 Southport 0

Havant&Waterlooville 5 Weymouth 0

Gosport Borough 2 Basingstoke Town 1 (*aet)

Didcot Town 0 Forest Green Rovers 3

Barnet 2 Concord Rangers 6

The last result on here, at first glance, looks like a real shock. Barnet are hoping to regain their League status this year, so to be hammered at home by a

Conference South side appears very strange. A quick check on the Barnet line-up however, revealed that Martin Allen, their experienced manager, played six players from their youth side. Getting a day out at Wembley is fantastic for the fans, but Allen was probably keen to avoid four further FA Trophy games for his starting eleven. Thus, the FA Trophy has, perhaps correctly, become a lower priority.

Last season, Gosport Borough made it to Wembley despite being a mid-table Conference South side, so I am beginning to think North Ferriby United might have a chance of progressing further than we initially thought and dare I say it, may even be an outsider for Wembley. Teams at the top of the Conference, like Barnet and Bristol Rovers, have already bowed out, so the most likely teams to reach the Final are the mid-table Conference sides who can afford to make it a serious priority. I keep, to Alan's annoyance, tipping Torquay United, as the 'Best Man' from our wedding, Andrew Berry, married Yvonne, a lady from Torquay and they live in Devon now. There often seems to be these quirks of fate on our journeys, so a trip to Torquay is in the back of my mind or even Andrew joining us at Wembley to watch Torquay.

There are several other teams remaining that catch the eye. As a Manchester City fan, Alan's worst case scenario is going to Wembley in March with tens of thousands of FC United of Manchester fans. His mate, Steve Mulligan, supports them, but I know Alan doesn't want them to win it. Looking at the bigger picture though, this book, with a 50p per sale donation to Manchester's specialist cancer hospital, 'The Christie' may benefit from a FC United of Manchester success. Not sure Alan will see it that way though.

From my perspective, Chorley are the team I most want to progress. I have lived in this town for thirteen years now and it would be wonderful if Chorley made it to Wembley as there would be hundreds of familiar faces cheering them on. Alan will no doubt be hoping Chorley at least manage to triumph in the Second Round, as they have been drawn at home to FC United. Others to note include Forest Green Rovers (as they hail from Nailsworth, Gloucestershire and I lived down in Gloucestershire for three enjoyable years), Altrincham (as Alan followed them for a season and blames himself for their relegation), Hemel Hempstead (as my grandfather's brother was player, coach, manager and secretary there) and Ebbsfleet United (as Peter Wanless, the Chief Executive of the NSPCC, who has read my two fictional books and I keep in touch with occasionally on Twitter, takes his son to watch them, so it would be good to meet him). I keep winding Alan up saying we will end up getting Dover Athletic v Torquay United in our two legged Semi Final. The other Semi would then end up being something like FC United against Altrincham, right on Alan's doorstep. It is wide open and with an attractive draw for the next round, I am sure Wembley is in the back of the minds of the players and officials at North Ferriby United. Having been in the Hull City end at Wembley last season, it would be surreal to be in the North Ferriby end in 2015.

"Don't get ahead of yourself, Cal," I can imagine Alan saying.

Tuesday 23rd December 2014

Finally the outstanding FA Trophy 1st Round games are underway. It's probably not been ideal for the players or supporters of the teams who have had to play games a couple of days before Christmas, but thankfully everything is sorted now and ready for the 2nd Round on the 10th January.

The outstanding results were as follows :-

Monday 22nd December

Chester 1 Telford United 1

(* after Extra Time the score remained 1-1. Telford won 4-3 on penalties.)

Tuesday 23rd December

Worcester City 0 Halifax Town 1

Welling United 2 Ebbsfleet United 3

(* after Extra Time. 2-2 after 90 minutes).

So, that's it for the FA Trophy for 2014. Roll on 2015 when Alan and I will once again be heading to Wembley. Wonder which teams will be coming with us? Could it be North Ferriby United? Merry Christmas!

Saturday 10th January 2015 – FA Trophy 2nd Round

North Ferriby United v Hyde

Attendance – 265

Happy New Year! Once again December was a month of over indulgence and January finds me weighing in at a portly sixteen stone once again. To try to shake off the excess flab, I am repeating last year's dry January but have added chocolate into the ban this year too.

For the second time, Jamie Lowe has decided to come with us to the game, so after picking Alan up at Buckshaw Parkway train station once again, at just after half ten, we head over to Jamie and Amy's in Brough, for lunch. Gale force winds were predicted by the tabloids, but the doom mongers over exaggerated their severity and it was a straight forward trip East.

When we arrived at Jamie's, Jamie and Amy were packing boxes as they are moving house at the end of January. Whilst packing, they managed to dig out a couple of books to lend to Alan and me. I had mentioned on Facebook, that I found Buddhism a fascinating religion, so would love to know more about it, so Amy passed me the only book on Buddhism she has. It's called 'Buddhism for Mothers' so may not be exactly the book I was looking for, but should give me a good grounding as to what the religion is all about. I am not intending to convert to Buddhism just to learn a little from Buddhist principles.

The book Alan borrowed from Jamie stemmed from a conversation about music that they had. Jamie was into the whole 'Madchester' scene far more than I was, when we were at Manchester Polytechnic and both Alan and Jamie went to the

Stone Roses Spike Island concert, so discussions about various Manchester bands took place over lunch. Jamie ended up lending Alan a book all about various bands from the Manchester scene in the early 1990's, which Alan scanned through and chatted away with Jamie about bands I had never even heard of.

After an hour and a half or so at Jamie's, we headed back over to North Ferriby for the third time. On arrival, we followed our usual routine of buying a programme each, buying raffle tickets each (which we never win) and then heading for the hot drinks trailer to buy coffees and oxo's. As I am off the beer, we skip heading into the bar for a pint and instead head over to the turnstile area by the far goal. As we were standing chatting an older gentleman, perhaps around sixty, came and stood by us, with a plastic bag in his hand. After listening in to our inane chatter for a moment or two, he asked me if I was Calvin Wade.

The gentleman in question was Trev Cunnington, who had added me as a Facebook friend the day before, but when I saw the friend request I hadn't appreciated why. I just added him, checked his profile to check he didn't appear to be a lunatic, which he didn't, he seemed like a music loving chap who had commented on a few things which gave me the impression he was a decent guy. Anyway, it turns out his son-in-law had bought him 'Another Saturday & Sweet FA' for Christmas and he had really enjoyed it. His son-in-law had heard me on BBC Radio Humberside with Andy Comfort so bought it for Trev for Christmas. Trev had noticed I was going to be at North Ferriby so had brought it with him to see if I would sign it.

People seem to like to have their books signed, which I am absolutely delighted to do. I have no delusions of grandeur which make me think it will ever be worth anything to have my signature in it, but if it adds something to the reader by me signing it, then I am happy to oblige. Alan signed it too. We chatted to Trev for a while and the impression he gives off on his Facebook page of being a good guy certainly seems to be right. He told me that when he read in the book about my Dad playing in an FA Cup 1st Round game between Scunthorpe United and Skelmersdale United, in December 1967, it took him right back, as he had been to watch that day and said he does remember it being freezing.

Whilst talking about my Dad and 1967, I need to temporarily do my Ronnie Corbett thing and go off on a tangent. It's an interesting one.

1967 FA Amateur Cup Final – Skelmersdale United v Enfield – Missing Medals

I haven't wanted to spend too much time in this book referring back to 'Another Saturday & Sweet FA', as I am assuming half the readers of this book, will have already read that book and half will not. I have tried not to repeat stories but it is worth pointing out that my Dad played in the 1967 FA Amateur Cup Final for Skelmersdale United against Enfield. They drew 0-0, 'Skem' missing a penalty in the last minute and Enfield won the replay at Maine Road 3-0.

This week my Dad, with three other former 'Skem' players have been at Goodison Park to acknowledge an act of kindness and generosity from one of the players in that Skem team to another. It also reflects an act of ineptitude and a lack of sentimentality from the FA.

Colin Bridge played left back in the Final. He had been a Skelmersdale United regular for five years and had played every game in every round 'Skem' had played in for five years on the trot. He picked up an injury in the final, however, and was replaced in the replay by Alan McDermott, who had been the substitute in the Wembley game. A member of the reserves, who had not been in the original twelve was drafted in as the substitute for the replay.

After Enfield won the Cup, as is still customary, the losing 'Skem' team were presented with their medals and then Enfield were presented with the Cup and their winning medals. Only twelve medals were handed out to each team, however and Colin Bridge, having missed the replay, found himself without a medal. Subsequently, Colin has contacted the Football Association on several occasions asking if he could have a medal. His requests have always been turned now.

Colin is 71 now and is in poor health as he has cancer. On becoming aware of Colin's illness, Alan McDermott made the decision to pass his Amateur Cup Final medal on to Colin. My Dad has always said Colin is the funniest man he knows and as a man who can put a smile on the face of others, it is fitting that in a troubled time, Alan has put a smile on Colin's face.

Feeling it was a newsworthy story, some of Colin's sporting friends such as former Liverpool legend, David Fairclough and Everton legend, Graeme Sharp arranged for Colin, Alan and some of their friends (which included two other Skem players from the Final, my Dad and Wally Bennett) to go to Goodison to take some photographs in the dressing room and on the pitch. Colin was a former Everton player before joining Skelmersdale, but had never made it to the first team. Stan Boardman, the Merseyside comedian and former Skelmersdale United player was also present, as he is a good friend of Colin's, as well as his son, former Sky Sports presenter, Paul Boardman.

My Dad said it was an excellent day out and Colin was in good spirits and could even make fun of his own illness.

"They have found a cure for cancer now," he announced.

"What's that, Colin?"

"Ebola!"

Ironically, Colin Bridge was not the only Skelmersdale United player who went to Goodison this week, who does not have an Amateur Cup medal to commemorate his appearance at Wembley. Wally Bennett had his medal stolen after a break in at his home and my Dad lost his when I was a small child. We had been on a family holiday and my Dad had put his medal, with some cash, in an envelope in a drawer for safe keeping. After we returned from the holiday, my Mum had decided to tidy around the house, including clearing out the drawer and had inadvertently thrown out the envelope that contained the cash and Dad's FA Amateur Cup Final medal. By the time my Dad realised it was missing, the binmen had already been to empty the bins and the medal was gone forever.

My Mum has always felt guilty about losing my Dad's medal, but she said what made her feel even guiltier was that my Dad didn't rant and rave about it. He was obviously upset that a treasured medal that signified the highlight of his footballing career had been lost but knew there was nothing he could do about it, so accepted it without the need for petty recrimination or shouting and bawling.

Wally Bennett not only lost his 1967 medal when his house was broken into, he lost a winners medal too. He played in the 1971 Amateur Cup Final for Skelmersdale United, this time winning the Cup in a 4-1 victory over Dagenham.

Many years later, someone mentioned to him that a friend had bought a 1971 FA Amateur Cup Final winners medal at a Sportsmans Dinner. Wally checked with the rest of the team and everyone else still had their own medals, so he knew it had to be his. He was then put in touch with the new owner and had to buy it back from him for a few hundred pounds.

North Ferriby United v Hyde (continued)

After Trev Cunnington went to watch the game from elsewhere, Jamie went into mickey taking mode about it being an honour to be watching the game with celebrities like Alan and myself. He always does things in a clever, quick witted way and soon had both Alan and myself chuckling. It is not really what Jamie says but the way in which he delivers it, that is funny. He is a naturally happy person and a joy to be around. In twenty five years of knowing him, I don't remember ever having a cross word with Jamie and the FA Trophy allowing us to spend time together has been an extra bonus. I was almost convinced before kick off, that this would be an easy victory for North Ferriby United, so in my mind, it was 50-50 that we would be back yet again, depending on whether North Ferriby were drawn at home or away for the last sixteen.

Our pre-match entertainment soon became even better. A coachload of Hyde fans positioned themselves right next to us and were soon in full voice. "Shit ground, one stand! Shit ground, one stand!" was the most repeated mantra. Hyde have had a tough time of things in recent seasons, finishing bottom of the Conference last season and are bottom of the Conference North, this season, but they have improved recently, with ex-manager, Gary Lowe, returning to the helm following the sacking of Scott McNiven. Last week, they drew 4-4 with high flying Barrow, coming back from 4-2 down to snatch a point.

"Have you been playing better recently?" I asked the teenage lad next to me.

"Not sure, I've only been to a couple of games," the lad replied.

"How come?" I questioned, assuming he normally followed City or United and had just come along with his mates.

"My Dad's only recently come back."

I put two and two together and for once, actually realised it was four.

"Is your Dad, Gary Lowe, the manager?"

"Yes."

Alan's ears pricked up and he joined the conversation with one of his typical, amazing groundhopping tales. It turns out Alan knew Gary Lowe from when he was manager of Curzon Ashton. Al had gone to watch them play at the now defunct Newcastle Blue Star and the game had been abandoned when part of the stand roof blew off.

"I remember that!" said Gary Lowe's son, but not excitedly, he was about eighteen and it isn't cool for eighteen year olds to look or sound excited unless they are drunk or sharing in some banter with their mates. He seemed like a decent lad though and was enjoying being with a gang of Hyde fans singing anti-Stalybridge Celtic songs, which also seemed to be common place.

One of the other songs the Hyde fans sang was "My Garden Shed Is Bigger Than This" mocking North Ferriby's relatively small ground. This being the fourth time we had seen North Ferriby, I noticed my brain switched into bias mode, as I thought,

'Yes, they are a village side with a small ground and in all likelihood after ninety minutes they will have beaten you. Let's see if you are singing then."

I am not knocking the Hyde fans, they were a lively bunch in high spirits and given the turmoil their club had been through, it was great they had brought a coachload along.

Most North Ferriby United fans are too long in the tooth for singing, but a small group of what appeared to be eleven and twelve year olds gathered beyond the nearest goal to us and started exchanging terrace chants with the Hyde contingent. A bizarre scene played out where forty grown men from Hyde attempted to out sing four primary school lads from North Ferriby. At one stage, the primary school lads sprinted towards us only to veer off to their left to go to play on the artificial pitch beyond the goal.

"Thank god for that! I thought they were charging us!" joked a beast of a Hyde fan who looked about eighteen stone of pure muscle.

Just before kick off, there was just time for Jamie to tell us an incredible story from when he was in his twenties. We were discussing the recent tragedies in Sydney and Paris when many innocent people had lost their lives due to the actions of crazed gunmen.

"Did I ever tell you about the time I had a gun pointed at me?" Jamie asked me.

"I don't think so," I replied.

Jamie then related a story from his days living in Manchester. A couple of years after we graduated from Manchester Polytechnic, Jamie found himself back in Manchester, as he worked for Makro. Originally he had started out as a Graduate Management Trainee in their store in Hull, but he was transferred, to do some work in their Head Office building in Manchester on the computer systems. Jamie moved into rented accommodation in Eccles. As he was so close to the City, friends would often come to stay for the weekend and Jamie would go with them into Manchester city centre to sample the delights of Manchester's nightlife.

One Saturday night, one of our friends from our Manchester Poly days, Lee Rankin, came to stay with Jamie and they went out to the pubs and clubs of Manchester. Lee is a brilliant character who we still keep in touch with to this day. He lives in Louth, Lincolnshire now, but is originally from Chorley. He is built like a Rugby League player and is a real man's man. He has worked throughout his career in the beer industry as a rep, an ideal job for a man who likes a drink and a cigarette himself. Lee always likes a laugh and a joke, but sometimes after a few pints too many, a stubborn, mischievous side to his character is displayed.

At the end of the evening, Lee and Jamie were trying to flag down a taxi and Lee was having a fag as they waited. A taxi pulled up and given it was the early 1990's, cigarette smoking had yet to be outlawed in public places, so Lee took his cigarette into the taxi with him.

"Can you put that out please, mate?" asked the taxi driver, as he started off towards Eccles.

"I will mate," Lee replied, "I'd near enough finished it anyway, I'll just have the last couple of drags and I'll be done."

It wasn't an unreasonable request but perhaps Lee wasn't thinking straight as the alcohol and nicotine flowed through his blood stream. He continued to smoke.

"Put it out," the taxi driver commanded, less politely second time.

Lee didn't pick up on the fact that the mood was changing.

"No problem, I'm near enough done, just one last drag."

Jamie said as Lee was enjoying one final drag of his cigarette, the taxi driver pulled over sharply, slammed on and immediately delved into his glove compartment. He turned around and pointed a gun at Lee and Jamie.

"I don't think you heard me properly, I told you to put it out. Get out my cab!"

Jamie said he had no idea if it was a real gun or not but he was not waiting to be asked twice and was out the taxi and 100 metres up the road quicker than Carl Lewis, but Lee calmly told the bloke to keep his hair on and slowly stepped out the taxi, finally stubbing his cigarette out as he did so. What's more, totally unphased, as the taxi driver span his cab around 180 degrees, frustrated that he had been dropped off a mile from the city centre and nowhere near Jamie's home, Lee went up and booted the side of the taxi. Only then did reality sink in and he then sprinted off down a side road before the taxi driver had time to retrieve his gun!

The following morning, Jamie said Lee joined him in the kitchen for a brew and asked,

"Did I dream it, or did some taxi driver threaten us with a gun last night?"

Once the game kicked off, all focus was on it. Hyde seemed like a very young side, but the programme notes indicated they had a few players who had been part of League club Academies, so they had good technical ability and sprayed the ball around well. The wind wasn't a force eight gale, but it was strong and the direction the corner flags were flapping, indicated it was on Hyde's backs and into the face of Adam Nicklin in the North Ferriby goal. Hyde didn't resort to long balls, although they did try to release Tom Bentham, their capable striker, who has an excellent scoring record despite playing for a bottom club side.

One of Hyde's best early chances fell to Luke Giverin, when he was released on the right edge of North Ferriby's box. Giverin is an ex Manchester United player, who had join their Academy as a seven year old and had stayed until released as a 20 year old in 2013. During his time at Manchester United, Giverin had been loaned out in late 2012, to second tier Belgian side, Royal Antwerp and had impressed them enough to be handed 24 first team appearances. Giverin shot across Nicklin, who had to launch himself acrobatically to get out an outstretched hand on the ball and palm it to safety. Hyde were definitely the better side in the early exchanges, as they tried to take advantage of the conditions being in their favour.

Billy Heath, the North Ferriby United manager, has put together a squad full of experience and we knew it would take a lot to break them down. Two of their most experienced players were actually missing. Danny Hone, an impressive centre back, who played professionally for Lincoln City, before they lost their League status, and most experienced of all, Adam Bolder, a combative midfielder who played over 150 games for Derby County and also played League football at a string of other clubs including Hull City, Queens Park Rangers and Millwall. Despite this, most of the Ferriby team have had some form of grounding at a League club, even if they did not make the first team. One of the exceptions is Louis Bruce, the right back who has come through the Youth system at North Ferriby, but has still had the experience of representing England at Under 18 Schools Level and at U19s College Level. Hyde's Connor Hughes was seen by many of the Hyde fans, next to us, as their main danger man, but Bruce was getting the better of their head to head battle.

As the first half progressed, despite the wind, North Ferriby United started to take control of the game. Hyde goalkeeper, Ashley Timms, seemed to be in good form though and made numerous strong saves, one with his legs to deny Jason St Juste, who was having another impressive game and a double save to deny Gregg Anderson's header and punching clear when the big stocky centre back, Mark Gray, looked poised to score from the rebound.

When the ref signalled it was half time, we headed around to buy a hot drink. As we had not edged around the ground during injury time, like we normally do, we were faced with a queue of about twenty people. For a change, rather than talk about football, Jamie and I were catching up on television programmes and films we had seen recently. Breaking Bad is both mine and Jamie's favourite television programme of all time and after discussing that briefly, we moved on to Homeland.

"Against the odds this fourth series has been superb, hasn't it?" Jamie commented.

"It has," I replied, "probably the best series yet. Peter Quinn, is one smooth bloke in it, isn't he?"

"He's brilliant. Carrie's great too."

"Did you know Rupert Friend, the lad who plays Quinn, is English really? He used to go out with Keira Knightley for years. If I was him, I'd adopt that American accent he does, as it's much smoother than his English one."

We were talking away like this and the lady in front of us, turned around and smiled.

"No offence intended, gentlemen, but you two sound like a pair of girls," she said.

"I know they do," Alan agreed, "that's why I was keeping out of the conversation."

The lady, whose name was Louisa, was really friendly and was soon joining in the conversation about films she liked, what was good on Netflix and what she had watched recently. It turned out she was the wife of Jason St Juste, the North Ferriby United left winger.

"You don't get to chat to the WAGs queuing for coffee at the canteen in the Premier League, Cal," Alan rightly pointed out, as we headed back around to our vantage point.

"Nor the son of the manager," I replied.

As the second half started, we strongly felt North Ferriby United would make better use of the wind than Hyde. I commented that I would be more than happy to go over to Hyde for a replay, but Alan, who had been there many times before, wanted a result. Despite Hyde being one of Alan's local teams, he wanted a result in North Ferriby's favour too. A lot of local teams to Alan had supported him on his fundraising mission with 'The Christie' but Hyde had not been one of them. Furthermore, when he had been to watch Hyde away at Blyth Spartans, in April 2010, Alan could only get a train ticket that would get him back into Manchester at 10:30 p.m, so to knock a few hours off his estimated arrival home time, he asked the programme editor if he could pay to get on the coach back. There were plenty of places, but the programme editor said he would need to have a word with the committee. After checking, he came back and told Alan that because he had not been on the coach on the way up to Blyth, there was no way they could allow him to be on the coach on the way back. In his years of groundhopping, Alan has been used to non-League teams going out their way to help him, so this negativity has always rankled with him and Hyde have become the local team he feels no allegiance to. Ironically, when the roof blew off the stand at Newcastle Blue Star when Gary Lowe had been manager at Curzon Ashton, he arranged for Alan to get on their coach home, so it is the committee rather than the managerial staff that Alan is not fond of.

Alan may not have wanted a draw but for much of the second half, it looked like Hyde were determined to get one. Sustained pressure from North Ferriby did not look like it was going to be enough, especially with Ashley Timms, the Hyde keeper, continuing the confident display that he had had in the first half.

Early in the second half, Louis Bruce hurled a long throw across aimed at Tom Denton and it was as accurate as a Fatima Whitbread javelin throw, dropping in the ideal spot for Denton to arch his neck and power a header towards goal, but Timms spread himself to make a comfortable save. Minutes later, Timms pushed a shot by the busy Ryan Kendall around the post and then Gregg Anderson headed over from the resultant corner. The pressure was building but it felt a little like Hyde could spring a major surprise with a smash and grab act, as in the rare moments they did break forward, their attackers looked lively. Connor Hughes escaped from Louis Bruce, for once, and forced an excellent save from Adam Nicklin. Whatever money North Ferriby United make from this cup run, Adam Nicklin should get himself an agent and claim a decent bonus, as whenever called upon he has made vital saves. Without the wonder penalty stop against Boston United at home, they wouldn't have even had a replay and then he performed very well in the replay and despite a relatively quiet afternoon, was doing so again. I have definitely seen less capable goalkeepers at much higher levels and if there is one player from the North Ferriby team who might have his finest days ahead of him rather than behind him, it would appear to be Nicklin.

After Nicklin's save from Hughes, North Ferriby United, began to press again. Liam King, who has captained the side for most games since Matt Wilson's sending off at Warrington Town, swept forward from midfield and sent a shot agonisingly wide. King is a small, busy midfielder, who reminds me in looks, physical frame and playing style of former Oldham Athletic central midfielder, Nick Henry, who formed a great central partnership with Mike Milligan in the Oldham heyday of the late 1980s and early 1990s. King looks more dangerous than Henry did going forward, as Henry lacked that goalscorer's instinct but other than that there are many similarities.

In a team that is not about individual brilliance and all about the whole being greater than the sum of the parts, in this FA Trophy, it is Adam Nicklin in goal and Tom Denton, up front, who seem to grab the majority of the headlines. When Nathan Peat, the substitute who had replaced Josh Wilde, sent a free kick sailing into the Hyde area in the 81st minute, it did not appear any more dangerous, than any previous ball into the box, but Denton manoeuvred himself to get his head onto it and from around penalty spot distance out, sent a looping header over the helpless Timms and into the back of the net. It was a heartbreaking moment for Timms who had done so much to keep North Ferriby United at bay, but Denton had registered his fourth goal in this season's Trophy, three of which, perhaps not surprisingly, had been headers.

Once the first goal went in, the Hyde team, as one, visibly sagged. Hyde had battled hard to make it a contest, but against such a well organised team as North Ferriby United, it appeared they lacked the self-belief to strike back. Rather than sit back and invite Hyde to come at them, North Ferriby continued to press and were rewarded in the final minute, when Liam King released Ryan Kendall as he made a diagonal run to his right. Kendall took the ball in his stride and struck a beautiful curling shot across the keeper and into the corner of the net. 2-0. Kendall, who has been battling for a regular position in the starting eleven was delighted and rightfully so, it was an exquisite finish that any Premier League striker would have been proud of. North Ferriby United were in the last sixteen.

After saying goodbye to Jamie, Alan and I headed back over the Pennines, chatting about whether we were going to witness an historic North Ferriby United Cup run. Since the FA Trophy returned to Wembley in 2007, it had been won by teams far bigger than North Ferriby United, teams like Stevenage, York City, Cambridge United and Wrexham have got their hands on the Trophy, so the chances of North Ferriby winning it, still seem very slim, but not impossible. When we saw Burscough win it in 2003, my Dad said a village team like Burscough would never win it again, could North Ferriby, twelve years later, prove him wrong? The draw on Monday will be an important one. A home draw or at least a draw that keeps North Ferriby away from a Conference high flyer and all of a sudden they may have a chance to avenge their Quarter Final defeat from last season. Roll on Monday!

FINAL SCORE :- North Ferriby United 2 Hyde 0

Other FA Trophy 2nd Round Results – Saturday 10th January 2015

Northern Section

Chorley 3 FC United of Manchester 3

Grimsby Town 0 Gateshead 0

Stockport County 2 Wrexham 2

Halifax Town 5 Alfreton Town 3

Kidderminster Harriers 0 Altrincham 1

AFC Fylde P Telford United P

Southern Section

Wealdstone 1 Bath City 3

Ebbsfleet United 1 Forest Green Rovers 0

Havant&Waterlooville 0 Dover Athletic 1

Maidenhead United 2 Farnborough 2

Gosport Borough 0 Braintree Town 2

Oxford City 2 Woking 2

Hemel Hempstead Town 3 Concord Rangers 1

Torquay United 4 Bromley 0

Burgess Hill Town 1 Dartford 2

The biggest disappointment for me from today's results was Chorley's failure to beat FC United of Manchester, drawing 3-3 at Victory Park. They now have an away leg to overcome at Curzon Ashton's Tameside Stadium on Tuesday night, with FC United probably slight favourites to progress. The dream Final would, from my perspective, be North Ferriby United against Chorley, although that would mean Alan and I would have seen North Ferriby in a minimum of eight games in the FA Trophy, prior to the Final, by then, so it would seem harsh changing allegiances to my hometown club. I am sure any bookmakers in the land would give me good odds on the Final being Chorley versus North Ferriby United.

After the last round, I mentioned five other teams who either Alan or I had an interest in, Torquay United, Forest Green Rovers, Altrincham, Hemel Hempstead Town and Ebbsfleet United. Of the five, only one, Forest Green Rovers, were knocked out. Forest Green were playing Ebbsfleet so one had to go.

Tomorrow's draw is the first one that ends the North-South split so we could end up anywhere. As I keep saying to Alan, it is a small country, so travelling anywhere on a Saturday is not really an issue, the issue would be heading to a remote part of the country for a Tuesday night replay. We would do it though.

Monday 12th January 2015 – Third Round Draw (Last 16)

Alan Oliver confused me this morning. If he ever needs a change of career, the BBC are still looking for a replacement for 'Mystic Meg' on the Lotto draw and after this morning's events, I am thinking Alan may fit the bill. When I checked Twitter at eight this morning, Alan had tweeted that it was Farnborough or Maidenhead United away for 'The Casual Hopper' and 'Calvin Wade'. Every other draw had taken place at midday Monday, so it seemed peculiar that the last 16 had been drawn earlier. Nothing else on Social media seemed to indicate an early draw so I thought no more about it, other than thinking perhaps Alan had his wires crossed and decided I would just check as usual at midday.

FA Trophy draws are always exciting on a Monday, but with it getting towards the final stages and with the potential of us heading anywhere in the country, this was a draw I was particularly looking forward to. I watched the North Ferriby United Twitter feed from twelve o'clock for any updates. Alan and I have become part of the social media North Ferriby United community now, having tweets regularly replied to and retweeted by their excellent 'Social Media Manager', John Rudkin. We haven't introduced ourselves to John yet, but he was taking photos behind the goal during the Hyde game and I intended to go and say hello, but he had moved on, by the time we headed for our half-time drink. John Colley, a North Ferriby United fan who has read 'Another Saturday & Sweet FA' and has become a real advocate for the book, doing whatever he can to help raise my profile around East Yorkshire, has said John Rudkin is a great guy, so I am looking forward to chatting to him. I would love to meet John Colley too, to thank him for all his help, but as yet, our paths haven't crossed as he does a 'Sales and Marketing' role for a self-storage firm called Armadillo and volunteer work for a local charity called 'Life For A Kid' so doesn't appear to get many free Saturdays. He is sponsoring a North Ferriby United game at the end of January and will be attending that game, but unfortunately it is the week after the FA Trophy. If North Ferriby United get to the Quarter Final and get a home draw, perhaps we will see him then.

Just after midday, the news came through. North Ferriby United have been draw away at Maidenhead United or Farnborough. After three home draws against Mickleover Sports, Boston United and Hyde, it seems like time for an away draw, but the fact that it turned out to be 'Maidenhead United or Farnborough' away, just like Alan had said at breakfast time, seemed very strange. Maybe the draw had taken place early this time. I rang Alan up.

"What's going on with this draw?"

"What do you mean, Cal?"

"How did you know the draw at eight o'clock this morning? Was it made then?"

"No."

"Then why did you tweet it being 'Maidenhead United or Farnborough' for us?"

"They are the only two grounds I haven't been to, mate. Why what's the draw?"

"Maidenhead or Farnborough."

"You're joking!"

"No straight up."

"Away?"

"Absolutely."

"That's fantastic."

After a brief chat with Alan, I had a look at how Farnborough and Maidenhead were fairing this season and then had a look on the map to see where Farnborough is. Alison, my wife, used to work for a pharmaceutical company that were based in Maidenhead, Berkshire, so I knew where that was. Farnbrough, it turns out, is in North East Hampshire. A check on AA Route Planner indicates that they are both about a four hour drive from Chorley.

With regards to current form, both Maidenhead United and Farnborough have had a tough season towards the lower end of the Conference South table. Maidenhead United are lower-mid table whilst Farnborough are in the bottom three. To give North Ferriby United the better chance of qualifying, I hope Farnborough win the replay, as on paper, they are the poorer of the two sides. I immediately check out the FA website and see that the replay is tonight. Given how dogged and determined North Ferriby United are as a team, I would expect them to get at least a draw against either of the two teams. Our adventure with North Ferriby United may well have life in it yet.

<u>10:00 p.m</u>

We are off to Farnborough for the last sixteen game. Tonight, Farnborough beat Maidenhead United 1-0, to ensure it will be them that host North Ferriby United on 24th January. I am pleased Alan gets to see a new ground in the last 16 and will check around to see if anyone might want to come with us. Gordon Johnson, the Liverpool County FA referee's Development Co-ordinator and Assessor may be a possibility as he was keen to get to a game during our FA Trophy adventures. My Dad definitely won't be coming as he is in Tenerife until the night before, but someone else might come forward unexpectedly. No matter what, Alan and I will be heading down to Farnborough a week on Saturday. I am looking forward to it already.

Other 2nd Round FA Trophy Results (Replays & Re-Arranged Game)

Tuesday 13th January 2015

FC United of Manchester 1 Chorley 0

Wrexham 6 Stockport County 1

Working 2 Oxford City 1

AFC Fylde P Telford P

Wednesday 14th January 2015

Gateshead P Grimsby Town P

Sad to see Chorley knocked out, so the dream final I mentioned between them and North Ferriby United is a non-starter already. Wrexham won it in 2013, and there was a bumper crowd of over 35 000 when they played Grimsby Town, so they will be in with a chance of winning it, despite having an indifferent season. From the start, Alan and I thought a mid-table Conference side would win, as the prize money isn't enough to entice the Conference high flyers to lose focus on promotion and if your team is towards the bottom of the Conference your team are probably not good enough to win it and your focus is on avoiding the drop. Our logic didn't apply last year though, as FA Trophy winners Cambridge United were doing well in the Conference too and ended up being promoted back to Division Two via the Play Offs.

I thought I would have a look to see what odds are available on each team left in the FA Trophy and they are currently as follows :-

F.C Halifax Town 6-1.

Torquay United 6-1.

Woking 7-1.

Wrexham 10-1.

Braintree Town 12-1.

Gateshead 12-1.

Grimsby Town 12-1.

Altrincham 14-1.

AFC Fylde 16-1.

Ebbsfleet United 16-1.

Dartford 20-1.

FC United of Manchester 20-1.

NORTH FERRIBY UNITED 20-1.

Bath City 25-1.

Hemel Hempstead Town 25-1.

Farnborough 33-1.

AFC Telford United 50-1.

North Ferriby United are one of the outsiders at 20-1 and are probably only as short in the betting as 20-1 because they play Farnborough in the next round, who are 33-1. One of the things I noticed when compiling the list, is that a few of these clubs have been dissolved and recreated. Halifax Town are now F.C Halifax Town, Farnborough Town are now Farnborough and Telford United are now AFC Telford United. Clubs at this level, like most levels outside the Premier League, are scrapping for survival and if the financial bonuses from the FA Cup aren't reaped, then the FA Trophy at least provides a reasonably healthy sum. North Ferriby United have already pocketed £15 000 from their three wins in the competition and for a small club like Ferriby, it is, I would imagine, a much appreciated cash injection. The real money is earned in the Final Stages though, as a minimum of £41 000 is gained from winning in the Semi Final (as your team receives £16 000 with a further £25000 going to the Runners Up and a further £50 000 to the winners).

Thursday 22nd January 2015

Gordon Johnson is coming with Alan and me down to Farnborough on Saturday. As an experienced former ref and retired policeman from Greater Manchester Police, I am sure he has a few interesting stories to tell. As he now works part-time for Liverpool County FA, he does a lot of assessing of referees so it will be good to hear what he makes of this Saturday's ref. I have known Gordon for several years due to his involvement in local football but more through mutual friends than knowing each other all that well, but Facebook has led us to become friendlier, as we have enjoyed following each other's footballing adventures. In 'Another Saturday & Sweet FA', I told a story about playing in a Sunday League game for a team called Metropolitan, with an average age of mid-30s, against the top of the League side who were all young lads and having one of the best games of my life to ensure a 3-3 draw. It turns out Gordon refereed that game. He also ran the line when I played against Everton for Burscough. Gordon was actually due to be at Finch Farm, Everton's training ground to co-ordinate the refereeing for the junior games this Saturday, but has asked someone to step in on his behalf.

Alan likes to keep a record of every ground he goes to and Gordon likes to keep a record of every match he officiated in (and who he booked and sent off) so I am sure there will be some common ground. I thought Gordon may be the first person to join us for a match who has been to more grounds than Alan, but it turns out Gordon is closing in on 300, whilst Alan is closing in on 400.

Today, bizarrely has seen another manager making strange comments to the press about North Ferriby United. Boston United manager, Dennis Greene had a pop at North Ferriby after the two FA Trophy clashes between the clubs and now

Farnborough manager, Spencer Day, has also passed comment, prior to his club's game with Ferriby.

Local Hampshire papers have commented that Spencer Day has said Farnborough literally face their "biggest test yet", as he called the North Ferriby United side "brutal" and "probably the biggest side he has ever seen". He also said they have a 6 feet 8 inch tall centre forward. From seeing them first hand four times already in the FA Trophy, I can honestly say none of this is correct. They have three or four options at centre back who are all tall, a very tall centre forward, Tom Denton, who is 6 feet 5 and a decent sized keeper, but the full backs, midfield and other strike options are not tall. In fact, as a team, I would be surprised if they have average 6 feet, with any combination of their squad.

As for the description of "brutal", I don't see where that has come from either. Danny Hone was sent off against Boston United, but that was only because ref, Michael Salisbury, correctly deemed him to be 'last man' when he committed the foul. As mentioned after the games against Boston United, they do have that Everton 'Dogs of War' mid-1990s quality about them, as they are fiercely competitive but not in a dirty way. They just work hard from front to back. I haven't witnessed them bullying refs by converging on them like some Premier League sides do, I haven't witnessed a barrage of bad language and I haven't witnessed mass penalty box wrestling from set pieces either. How being well drilled and competitive has led them to be deemed as 'BRUTAL GIANTS', I really don't know.

Saturday 24th January 2015 – FA Trophy 3rd Round

Farnborough v North Ferriby United

Attendance – 391

I haven't been this excited about going to a game since the FA Cup Quarter Final last year between Arsenal and Everton. The neutrality thing has gone out the window now and I desperately want North Ferriby United to make it to Wembley. I know it's probably an unrealistic wish but to see them get to Wembley having watched them every step of the way, would be amazing. It would make a great story for the book too. Realistically, Farnborough, with their lowly current League position are even less likely to make it to the Final so we are not likely to see any other winner of the Competition more than three times. If North Ferriby get to Wembley, we will have seen them at least nine times.

After driving Joel around his paper round (a routine I have said will stop come 1st March), I nipped back home, dropped Joel off, said goodbye to Alison and Brad, collected my coat and wallet and headed off to Buckshaw Parkway to pick Alan up. From there, we picked Gordon up at Wrightington, just off the M6 and drove down to Farnborough.

As expected, Alan and Gordon got on famously. As people, they are very different, but their passion for football is very similar. Once they get talking, Alan immediately suspects that he will have been to a game that Gordon has refereed and he determinedly tries to find one. Alan quizzes Gordon about grounds he has been to and when, looking for that elusive link. Failing to find one, Alan begins to tell Gordon about arrangements he is putting in place for a game in May at Droylesden between Manchester City Supporters Club and a Manchester City former players team. Alan explains that this will be the second time the game has taken place, after a successful game took place last season which raised thousands for 'The Christie'.

"I've reffed the Manchester City Former Players XI team, last season, at Prescot Cables Hope Street ground for the Bert Trautmann Memorial game against St Helens Town," explains Gordon.

"That's it!" Alan said excitedly, like a man who had solved a puzzle, "that's the game I've been to when you've reffed. I was at that game!"

Many stories are then traded on the long journey down. Alan warns Gordon to remember that I note everything mentally so if there are stories he doesn't want to appear in the pages of my book, then he needs to warn me. Gordon tells a great one about his night at the Professional Football Association Awards dinner, some years ago.

"Can I put that in the book, Gordon?"

"No!"

Damn.

The reason we were discussing the PFA, was because Gordon Taylor, the Chief Executive of the PFA has made comments this week, making comparisons between Ched Evans, the disgraced former Sheffield United player, who is fighting his conviction for rape and the families of the victims of the Hillsborough tragedy. At best, it was a misguided analogy and mistimed too. If Ched Evans is found to be innocent through the Courts of Appeal, then his quest for justice might have a very tenuous link to the families of the Hillsborough victims, but as things stand, he is a convicted rapist and to make any links to the Hillsborough families seems to me to be very wrong and a not unexpected public outcry has taken place.

We stopped an hour from Farnborough for a spot of lunch at a roadside restaurant, not a Little Chef, but something similar. Whilst there, Alan asked Gordon if he would referee this year's Charity football match for 'The Christie' that they were discussing earlier and Gordon kindly agreed. Forgetting my age and my propensity to get injured easily, I offered my services as a goalkeeper, for a brief appearance. As soon as I said it, I started to regret it and will probably back out before May comes around. I am 44 next Friday, have bad knees, dodgy hamstrings and I'm carrying too much weight, but know if you put me between two sticks I will be diving around like a madman.

We arrived at Farnborough at about one o'clock. We parked a few hundred metres down the road and walked up. If any of the three of us had been there before, we would have realised there is a massive, free car park just outside the ground, but we hadn't so we walked up. We took a few photos outside the ground and then spotted the bar entrance so headed in there for a pre-match drink. I would have loved to have had a nice, cold pint after a four hour drive, but as I am off the ale again for January, I had to give it a miss.

The bar was full of officials from both clubs and a coachload of North Ferriby United supporters proudly kitted out in their green and white club colours. Having been two of the ten away supporters at Boston United, it was great to see that North Ferriby had brought a much better following to this game. As we started our drinks, I pointed out to Alan that John Rudkin, the Social Media Manager of North Ferriby was ten yards away and that I was going to have a word with him once I'd had a few crisps and a slurp of my drink.

"Which one is he?" Alan asked.

"The bald headed bloke over there," I said pointing over.

Alan didn't really look at where I was pointing and being the type of person who likes to act in the moment, rather than wait patiently, strode across.

"Are you John Rudkin?" he asked another bald headed bloke in the North Ferriby party, who we later discovered is Chris Norrie.

"No," Chris and I said simultaneously, "John's that bloke over there."

I went over with Alan and we introduced ourselves to John.

John Rudkin is a very friendly man with an infectious laugh and was well aware of us through our social media contact with him. He was also an inside track to find out a few things about what was going on at North Ferriby. John's a former goalkeeper and after he packed in, wanted to continue an involvement with non-League football. Despite being from Scunthorpe, it transpired North Ferriby United were the club for him. Three years into following North Ferriby and half a season into his role as 'Social Media Manager', he is loving it.

"What's happened to Jamie Yates?" I asked John.

The former Boston United player, who had been taken off injured at half-time at Boston, after receiving consistent abuse from the sidelines, has never reappeared since, as far as I was aware. He seemed a good player, so his disappearance had puzzled me.

John explained that after the injury at Boston, Jamie made one more substitute appearance at Gloucester City and then returned last week to his former club, Gainsborough Trinity. There may well have been more to it, that John either did not know or did not reveal, a fall out, a concern that he was not going to command a regular place, but whatever the reason, it seemed to me like Jamie Yates was sacrificing a potential Wembley place. Perhaps that view is me being optimistic on Ferriby's behalf and Yates being a pragmatist, but as a player, if I ever had a sniff of Wembley, I would not be changing clubs.

I also went on to ask about Matt Wilson. The season had started very brightly for him when he scored the only goal in front of 2714 supporters at Stockport County, but subsequently the Warrington Town sending off and the substitution against Mickleover Sports have seemingly led to his season fizzling out. He started the season as club captain too, but was replaced by Russell Fry and then midfield dynamo Liam King took over. John thinks Wilson has just been unfortunate with injuries and suspension and believes he is back challenging for a place for today's game.

John had travelled down the night before with some of the North Ferriby United board and the team. Some of the team, due to work commitments had to follow down in their own cars a few hours after the team coach left, but they had had an enjoyable evening, the players having a quiet night whilst John said he had over indulged a bit and was nursing a slight hangover. They were quietly confident of victory and I said I was confident they would win comfortably too, whilst John said he would be happy for a draw, a victory at home on Tuesday and Bath City at home in the Quarter Finals.

I also asked John what his take was on the comments from Farnborough manager, Spencer Day, about the team being "brutal" and "the biggest team he had ever seen". John thought it was all very strange but said that all at North Ferriby, including the players, were delighted that the Farnborough manager had seemingly instilled a bit of fear into his own camp. When they had arrived at the ground, North Ferriby had organised their players so all the tallest lads came off the coach first!

After a very enjoyable chat, we left John with the rest of the party from North Ferriby United and Alan, Gordon and I headed into the ground. Farnborough FC, very much like Boston United, have had a chequered recent history. At one stage, it had promised so much but had now left them with so little.

Farnborough FC were created after the former Farnborough club, Farnborough Town were dissolved in 2007. Farnborough Town were not an ancient club themselves, starting in 1968, in the Surrey Senior League. They made steady progress up the pyramid system and in the 1988-89 season finished runners up in the Isthmian League Premier Division and after the Champions Leytonstone failed to meet the specifications to join the GM Vauxhall Conference, Farnborough Town were invited to be promoted in their place. They were relegated in their first season in the top flight of non-League football, but immediately bounced back and achieved a promotion to enable them to start the 1991-92 season in the Conference once more. They finished in 5th place in the Conference but the following season were relegated again and Ted Pearce, who had managed the club since 1970 stood down.

The rest of the 1990's saw a further promotion back to the Conference, five years of stability within it, generally finishing mid-table, then a further relegation, followed in 1999, by the arrival of a character we had come across last year during our FA Cup travels, the now Stevenage manager, Graham Westley. He took over Farnborough Town on all fronts in 1999, becoming both owner and manager.

In 2001, Westley guided Farnborough Town back to the Conference once again. The following season, they finished 7th in the Conference and the year after that 2002-03, Farnborough Town had the biggest game in their history when they were drawn to play Arsenal in the FA Cup 4th Round. Controversially, the tie was moved to Highbury and Arsenal won 5-1, which turned out to be Westley's last game in charge, as he resigned to join Stevenage Borough who he believed had better long-term prospects. Westley had not always been a popular figure at Farnborough Town, as he had tried to organise a merger with Kingstonian, which failed and had dismantled his promotion winning 2000-01 side after they had been promoted to the Conference. His legacy was further dented when he took seven Farnborough players to Stevenage with him and withdrew his financial backing of the club.

In a strange twist of fate, Westley passed the ownership of the club to Vic Searle who further down the line became owner-manager too. The twist of fate being that when Searle became manager, the Assistant was Ken Charlery, who had been a player at Boston United during the Steve Evans contract discrepancy era too. A rocky five years followed with regular boardroom wrangles and various managers taking the helm. The ownership battles eventually led to the club facing a winding up order from the Inland Revenue in July 2006, with debts of over £1 million pounds. The club failed to survive after a protracted period of negotiations and were liquidated with Farnborough FC rising from the ashes.

Farnborough FC paid the price for the failure of Farnborough Town and had to begin life two levels below Farnborough Town, beginning in Southern League 1 South & West Division. Owners and managers continued to change but progression was made and by the start of the 2010-11 season, Farnborough were back in the Conference South.

If you managed to follow all the above, you will have realised Farnborough/Farnborough Town have had a turbulent existence, but it became a bizarre one when Paddy Power bookmakers became involved with the club. Paddy Power have a comical and unorthodox way of advertising their firm and when they began a business relationship with Farnborough, in 2013, they decided they could grab some press headlines by bringing a squad of some of the greatest footballing names of all time to Farnborough. The plan wasn't to spend hundreds of millions on some of the world's finest players, it was to change the names of the existing squad, by deed poll, to those of famous footballers past and present.

Paddy Power saved Farnborough from administration when they became the main sponsors of the club, but how manager Spencer Day felt about changing his name to Jose Mourinho, the goalkeeper, Kevin Scriven, having his name changed to Gordon Banks and others to the likes of Zidane, Gascoigne, Lineker, Messi, Maradona and Pele, I really don't know. Obviously by changing their names, this allowed the players to have their new, all star, surnames on the back of their Farnborough shirts.

The gimmick was an amusing one, but the officials who ran Conference South failed to see the funny side. Farnborough were told in no uncertain terms that unless the names were changed back to the original players names, Farnborough would be refused entry to the League.

Paddy Power himself commented,

"We didn't think it was possible to match our unveiling of the greatest XI the world has ever seen for Farnborough FC, but the Football Conference has trumped us by revealing the greatest sense of humour failure of all time!

He continued: "Since the sponsorship was announced, the Football Conference have proved themselves to be nothing more than miserable, Grade-A bullies. It seems to us that they would have rather seen Farnborough FC down and out than embrace the idea of Messi, Pele and Mardona driving worldwide interest and fun for Conference football. Farnborough FC have finally been allowed to start their season and do so with our full support."

Still, the whole thing managed to get the bookmakers a lot of publicity with their innovative move and it also saved the relatively new club from potentially dropping out of existence once more. The stadium is still called 'The Paddy Power Stadium' and when we entered it, we were very impressed with how great it looked. The team are struggling, which is a shame, as, according to the fans, the club is still cash strapped, but it is a stadium that would grace Division One or Two.

Gordon took his camera with him so was wanting to take as many photos as he could. We circled the ground, taking photos from all angles. He has a bit of a dry sense of humour (which I wouldn't imagine is unusual for refs or policemen) so had us sitting down for photos below 'No Standing' signs and peering above barriers behind 'No Entry' signs. Gordon was also interested in watching the ref and his assistants warm up and was not impressed to see one of the assistants warming up with a hat on.

"If you aren't going to wear it during the match, don't wear it in the warm up," Gordon muttered disapprovingly.

"Why would you not want him to?" Alan asked with interest.

"Well, my view is that as a ref or assistant ref, you want to draw as little attention to yourself as possible, it's easy enough to get stick from the sidelines anyway, so wearing a hat in the warm up or tracksuit bottoms, is a non-starter as far as I'm concerned."

Gordon is a jovial man and Alan pointed out he was the ideal replacement for Jamie as they are both quick witted and cheerful, but at 6 feet 2, stocky build and strong minded, you wouldn't want to get on the wrong side of him on a football pitch or be slung into a cell by him, for that matter. I knew it was going to be interesting watching the game with him, as he would see things that Alan and I would normally fail to spot.

When the teams came out to shake hands and do the final pre-match warm up, we were particularly interested in what the North Ferriby United team was. Danny Hone was back after six games out the side, due to suspension and then not being immediately able to force his way back, due to the solid form of Gregg Anderson and Mark Gray, the other centre backs. Anderson and especially Gray, have a look of American football linemen, stocky and robust, but Hone has always appeared to be blessed with an extra yard of pace and perhaps has been brought back to try to counter the threat posed by Farnborough striker, Louie Theophanous, who has apparently scored eight goals in his last eight games, an especially impressive statistic given the club's current plight. Other than in the centre of defence, the team is the same as against Hyde.

When the game started, Farnborough began strongly. Farnborough's midfield looked dangerous going forward and they were seeking out the hungry Theophanous, who had a well struck shot saved by the ever dependable Adam Nicklin in the seventh minute. Five minutes later, Theophanous was put clear of an unusually static Ferriby defence and as he raced through, I was fully expecting him to put Farnborough one-up. Perhaps his recent goalscoring feats have allowed Theophanous to become a little too confident, as rather than picking his spot, he tried to round Nicklin and stroke the ball into an empty net. Nicklin was alert to the danger and pounced, cat like, at his feet to collect the ball. Having seen North Ferriby on a number of occasions, we knew they would get back into the game and Farnborough could be left to rue important missed opportunities. A further shot on goal from the impressive, fast striker, Reece Beckles was again saved well by Nicklin.

Jason St Juste, the North Ferriby United is also quick and difficult to handle and he went on a marauding run along the left wing that was brought to a stop by a late challenge from Farnborough's Jamie Hand that earned the defender a booking. Hand looked like the experienced figure amongst a team of largely young players with experience of League football at Watford, Oxford, Peterborough and Northampton amongst others, but into his thirties now, he would need all his experience to deal with the tricky St Juste.

Hand's tackle was immediately punished when Russell Fry sent over an inch perfect ball into the box that was met by a thumping near post header from the 6 feet 5 inch striker, Tom Denton. Farnborough had continued to describe him as over 6 feet 8 inches tall in their press articles and he must have appeared at least that tall to the Farnborough centre backs, as he is so difficult to combat in the air. Against the run of play, after nineteen minutes, North Ferriby United were one-nil up. We were stood at the halfway line amongst the Farnborough fans, so didn't celebrate, Alan and I just exchanged a 'we're not surprised' look.

Sometimes, when teams are struggling, heads drop when they go behind, but Farnborough continued to press forwards with intent. Lloyd Foot, the Farnborough captain, had a shot from a tight angle that hit the side netting at Nicklin's right hand post. Some Farnborough fans thought on the far side of the ground thought it had crept in and began to celebrate, but were soon disappointed to see Nicklin place the ball for a goal kick. Nicklin was soon back in action with a further save from Reece Beckles.

North Ferriby United had weathered the early storm though and their midfield began to get into the game. Danny Clarke wasn't having his best ever half, struggling a little with his close control, but he worked tirelessly up and down the right wing to cut out Farnborough attacking options down the left and continued to provide an outlet going forward. Liam King, who had been very quiet in the opening twenty minutes, started to come into the game and looked to release Clarke, St Juste and the lively Ryan Kendall.

It was a clear, cold day and Alan noticed the floodlights had been on throughout.

"What are the floodlights for?" he complained.

"Oh, they are used to light the pitch up. I'm surprised you've never noticed them before Al," Gordon replied with a smile.

On the half hour mark, another Russ Fry set piece, this time a corner, was again met by Tom Denton, but this time he flicked it on, to a gleeful Ryan Kendall who finished from close range with a back post header. 2-0.

"It's not as though they weren't warned," Alan commented.

He was right. Farnborough had clearly identified that Tom Denton was a danger man, but it's easier to be aware of his threat than to counter it. Although Farnborough heads did not go down after the first goal, they seemed to after the second. "Brutal" may not have been the right word to describe North Ferriby United, 'clinical' may have been more accurate but they had certainly delivered two sucker punches. It must have been hard to take for the young Farnborough side, but we were learning that North Ferriby United's sum was definitely greater than their individual parts. They may not be the best eleven players in the world, but they epitomised the word 'team'. Billy Heath, the manager, had assembled a side that were not going to go out this competition without a fight.

Half time arrived and the score was still 2-0. We were convinced that was it, North Ferriby United were through. Every game we had seen them take the lead in, they had gone on to win convincingly. Alan and I were not North Ferriby United fans when the FA Trophy began, but we were starting to get the feeling that we were witnessing something special. Less than 4000 people live in North Ferriby village and for them to reach the Quarter Final two years on the trot, is pretty amazing. Who knows, they might even go further this year.

Over a cup of tea, we discussed Farnborough's slim chance. The only way we could see them getting back into it, would be if they scored before the hour mark. Perhaps we were being premature to have automatically given North Ferriby United a pass to the Quarters, I am sure Billy Heath didn't have that attitude in the dressing room, but things were looking incredibly promising.

We also had a chat with Gordon about the performance of the referee, David Rock. He felt he was doing a very good job. He felt the Assistant Referee may have missed one marginal offside against Farnborough, but all major decisions had been right and the ref had allowed the game to flow when given the opportunity.

When the players came out for the second half, Ryan Kendall, who had had a busy first half, was missing and had been replaced by experienced hand, Adam Bolder.

"Kendall must be injured," Alan observed.

Billy Heath, the North Ferriby United manager, may look like a nightclub doorman, tall, stocky, bald and a man not to be messed with, but he has a wealth of non-League managerial experience and it soon became obvious that Kendall was probably not injured as Ferriby lined up with a 4-5-1 formation. Farnborough had been breaking through midfield and Heath put Bolder into a central midfield three to tighten things up.

It was a shrewd move and Farnborough were stifled. With Tom Denton lacking pace, he could well have been sacrificed as Kendall has more pace to chase down any cleared balls, but Denton is useful defensively, especially from set pieces as he can drop deep and extinguish the aerial threat. With Farnborough sensing their chance was gone, Ferriby looked the more likely side to add to the goal tally, Liam King, Danny Clarke and Adam Bolder all went close in the first ten minutes of the second half. After that, it became a bit of a stalemate. The first half had been lively, the second half became dull, but this suited North Ferriby, as they were ensuring a trouble free passage to the Quarter Finals. With around ten minutes to go, Farnborough had one final chance, Reece Buckles once again did well to beat the offside trap, but, as ever in the Trophy, Adam Nicklin was alive to the danger and raced off his line to win another one-on-one, spreading himself to make the save.

After that it was plain sailing. Farnborough fans began to dejectedly head towards the exits and the Ferriby fans that had made the long trip from East Yorkshire, began to sing, dance and wave their banners, in the massive 1500 seater stand behind the Farnborough goal. After a couple of minutes of injury time, the ref blew the whistle to confirm a result that had never looked in doubt after the second Ferriby goal went in. North Ferriby United, for the second successive year, had made it to the FA Trophy Quarter Final.

During injury time we had started heading around to the North Ferriby United fans behind the goal, from our vantage point on the halfway line. Once the whistle blew, the Ferriby players headed over to their small band of fans near us. Alan, who had managed to keep his neutrality throughout fourteen rounds of the FA Cup, found he had now become, on this Trophy trail, a North Ferriby United "Villager".

"Oi, Tom!" he shouted over at Tom Denton, before pumping his fist and snarling his face in delight.

Tom Denton looks perpetually bemused on the football pitch and this was no different. He didn't have a clue who this small, stocky, baldy Mancunian was and just stared back vacantly. If Ferriby keep winning, he might have to get used to seeing Alan celebrating on the touchline. We didn't come into this wanting Ferriby to win it, but we are firmly behind them now.

As we walked to the exit, we saw John Rudkin and his partner, Julie. John spends most of each game stood pitch side with a camera in his hand taking photos for the club and this was the case again today.

"We made hard work of it first half, but we shut up shop second half. It was a good professional display. Let's see who we get next round on Monday now. Hope we're at home," John said, with a look of satisfaction on his face.

We wished him and Julie a safe trip home and then we were set off back towards the car. Gordon had taken a huge amount of photos too and said he would upload them on to Facebook before the weekend was out. He was just disappointed that work commitments for Liverpool County F.A meant he didn't think he'd be able to get to the next couple of rounds.

The drive back from Farnborough was a long one, but both Alan and Gordon are always good company so time flowed a lot quicker than if I was on my own. It was made a particularly interesting journey because it has been a sensational day in the FA Cup.

There have been some massive shocks in the FA Cup 4th Round. I won't dwell on them all, because this is an FA Trophy story this year, not an FA Cup one, but just want to mention a couple. Bradford City, a League One side, beat Premier league leaders, Chelsea, 4-2 at Stamford Bridge after Chelsea had gone 2-0 up. It is being described as one of the biggest shocks of all time. One of the Bradford City players (and scorers) Filipe Morais, played for Stevenage when we saw them three times in the FA Cup last year. He scored the equalising goal. Both Morais and Luke Freeman stood out at Stevenage so it isn't surprising that both have remained in League One after Stevenage's relegation to League Two.

The second biggest shock, which dampened Alan's mood on the journey home a little, was Middlesbrough's shock 2-0 win over Manchester City. Both Everton and Manchester City made it to the Quarter Finals when we were on our FA Cup trail last season, but this year Everton were knocked out by West Ham in the 3rd Round and City have lost to Boro in the 4th. A good year to do the FA Trophy instead.

We listened to the Liverpool – Bolton five thirty kick off as I drove back, which wasn't the most exciting game to listen to as it finished goalless. This year's FA Cup is being touted as an opportunity for Steven Gerrard, who is leaving Liverpool at the end of the season to join LA Galaxy, to sign off with an FA Cup winner's medal. I still expect them to overcome Bolton in the replay but today's results have shown anything can happen.

After a long drive, I dropped Alan off at Crewe railway station and Gordon off at the spot I'd picked him up at, in Wrightington. Gordon wished us well in the remaining rounds and said he may well go to Wembley for the Final. It would be brilliant if he did.

An exciting Monday morning awaits now, to see where North Ferriby United are heading next in the midday draw. In every Round so far, North Ferriby United, it could be argued, have had an element of good fortune with the draw and have been favourites to progress but at the Quarter Final stage, they are unlikely to be favourites. North Ferriby United progressing this far in the FA Trophy, is probably equivalent to a club like Brentford getting to the Quarter Finals in the FA Cup. By which, I mean a small club that are in the second top flight, who punch above their weight, who have done well to reach the latter rounds but who are not realistically expected to go all the way. I keep telling Alan that Torquay United await, so let's see if the next round takes us to the seaside. We certainly can't seem to shake off North Ferriby United, these 'brutal giants' keep on winning.

FINAL SCORE :- Farnborough 0 North Ferriby United 2

Other FA Trophy Third Round Proper Results

North Ferriby United were one of only four teams to guarantee a place for themselves in the Quarter Finals, as the other results today were as follows :-

Wrexham 1 Gateshead 1

FC Utd of Manchester 3 AFC Fylde 1

Dartford 2 FC Halifax Town 2

Hemel Hempstead Town 0 Torquay United 2

Bath City 1 Altrincham 0

Woking 3 Dover Athletic 3

Braintree Town P Ebbsfleet United P

I guess I prematurely gave the game away that Torquay United had won but of the other results, there were a couple of 'shocks', FC United of the Evo-Stik Premier beating AFC Fylde who are table topping in the Conference North, one League above them. Bath City of Conference South are also a League below Altrincham of the Conference. I would say from a North Ferriby United perspective, an away draw against a Conference side would test them to the limits, whilst a home draw against a side they are on a par with, like Bath City or in a League above, like FC United of Manchester, would be very welcome indeed.

Monday 26th January 2015 – FA Trophy Quarter Final Draw

Last year, when the FA Cup draw took place on ITV, I'll always remember Alan saying that as the draw was made, it almost felt like we were part of it. Whatever number ball was attributed to the club we followed, felt like 'our ball'. We didn't obviously feel like players, but certainly felt, albeit temporarily, that we somehow belonged to that club. That feeling is back today. I think the Boston United manager, Dennis Greene, played a part in our affiliation to North Ferriby United, as once he started having a go at their style and tactics, it seemed only natural to come down on Ferriby's side.

If North Ferriby United can somehow manage to get past two more clubs, they will walk out at Wembley on Sunday 29th March and we will have seen every single minute of their FA Trophy campaign. I have checked the odds and bookmakers are now offering around 12-1 for North Ferriby United to win the Trophy. I wonder what odds they were at the start of the tournament? I would guess about 66-1.

The draw was delayed today so rather than announce it at midday, news came out at about quarter past. The draw was as follows :-

FA Trophy Quarter Final Draw

Dover Athletic or Woking v Bath City

FC Halifax Town or Dartford v Wrexham or Gateshead

Torquay United v FC United of Manchester

North Ferriby United v Braintree Town or Ebbsfleet United

My immediate thoughts about the draw are all over the place. Firstly, it's a great draw for North Ferriby United. A home draw must have been the dream, their home record is a great deal better than their away, they have only lost once at home all season in all competitions, back in early September against Solihull Moors when the team had a few different players and were in the midst of a poor run that saw them only win one in seven. Since then, they have played 13 more home games and lost none. Secondly, if it's Ebbsfleet United, then it would be great to meet Peter Wanless, the NSPCC Chairman who has read my two fictional books and him and his 13 year old son are both reading "Another Saturday & Sweet FA" at the moment. Thirdly, a replay in Kent or Essex on a Tuesday night would be a bit of a nightmare!

This will be our fourth trip to North Ferriby and once again gives me the opportunity to call in on Jamie. I will also see if my Dad fancies coming to this one as he did say that he would come to a game and if Braintree or Ebbsfleet emerge victorious from the Quarter Final, I can't see him fancying the trek down there. I remind myself to think positive, North Ferriby United have a real chance and if they do win, we would have a fifth trip to Ferriby for one of the Semi Final legs. Now wouldn't that be amazing?

I speak to Alan. 'The Casual Hopper' aka 'The Mancunian Villager' is delighted Ferriby have a home draw. He thinks it will be Ebbsfleet United despite Braintree being at home in the re-arranged game tomorrow night. Like me, he is starting to think North Ferriby United have a chance to re-write their record books and is excited that we have managed to follow them throughout. I tell him to have a glance at the Manchester United v Liverpool U21s game at Leigh Centurions tonight as it is being refereed by Michael Salisbury, my sons PE teacher who was the man in the middle for the first North Ferriby-Boston game. I think it's on SKY but I'm not sure Alan has SKY. I'm sure he's not going to journey out to the pub for it.

At the Quarter Final stage of the FA Cup last season, it reached its peak, from a personal perspective, as the side I was desperate to win, Everton, the team I have always supported were knocked out by Arsenal. I am hoping the FA Trophy doesn't go the same way. If North Ferriby United are knocked out, following Braintree Town or Ebbsfleet United won't have the same feel. We don't have the time to get to know their players, officials or fans. I think I could identify all the North Ferriby United squad now, which is not something I ever thought would happen.

I have contacted Peter Wanless and if Ebbsfleet United get past Braintree Town, he doesn't think he would travel up to North Ferriby but hopes he gets to see me either in a replay or in the home Semi Final leg. I would love to meet Peter and his son, but if it means sacrificing North Ferriby United, I think I would rather opt for seeing him next season in the FA Vase instead. His boyhood team were Chippenham Town, so heading down there would be great. In all likelihood though, I have a feeling our paths will cross this year. Footballing fate seems to conspire to bring me together with people who have a story to tell, so my money is on Ebbsfleet United beating Braintree Town, Ferriby and Ebbsfleet drawing and us meeting Peter Wanless and his son on a cold Tuesday night in Kent!

Tuesday 27th January 2015

Nothing has happened tonight to alter the view that Alan and I will be heading down to Ebbsfleet United at some point. Braintree and Ebbsfleet played out a 1-1 draw tonight, so will replay next Tuesday at Ebbsfleet. I spoke to Alan and he is 100% sure it will be Ebbsfleet now. In fact, he is so convinced, he is going to head down to watch the Conference South game between Gosport Borough and Ebbsfleet United on Saturday, on a spying mission.

With my finances being tight, I don't tend to go to any other games except the FA Trophy ones, but Alan is trying to get to 400 grounds this season by completing all the grounds in the League of Wales and also getting to as many Conference South grounds as he can. Gosport Borough is one he has yet to tick off and it particularly appeals as the quickest way to get there for a non-driver like Alan, is to get down to Portsmouth and then catch a ferry to Gosport. Al says he's never taken a ferry to a game before, so he is looking forward to it. Will be interested to see what he makes of Ebbsfleet United and also whether anyone at North Ferriby United will take note of his observations.

The other result tonight saw Dover Athletic triumph 1-0 over Woking to become the fifth team to book their Quarter Final slot. I have been saying to Alan for some time that we would end up with a Dover-Torquay semi-final but thankfully that isn't possible now, as one of North Ferriby, Braintree or Ebbsfleet will be our Semi Final representative. This does mean, however, that we could still have two semi finals, one Saturday after the other in Essex and Devon or Kent and Devon. Yet another reason to want North Ferriby United to make it through. The other replay that was due tonight between FC Halifax Town and Dartford was postponed. For geographical reasons, we could do with Halifax winning that one too.

Wednesday 28th January 2015

Tonight's game between Gateshead and Wrexham has been postponed because the pitch is waterlogged. The game has been re-arranged for next Tuesday, as has the Ebbsfleet United – Braintree replay and the FC Halifax Town – Dartford one. If the ties don't take place next Tuesday, they will take place on the Saturday, which means the Quarter Final games will be put back. Braintree Town have a pitch that seems to waterlog from time to time, but now the tie is at Ebbsfleet, we may be alright. We have been very lucky so far to avoid postponements in our games and John Rudkin at Ferriby said,

"We don't do postponements at North Ferriby United."

So hopefully if the last 16 game takes place next Tuesday, we will be fine for the Quarter Final on Saturday. There's some bad weather due in the next ten days, so just watch it get postponed now I've written that!

Saturday 31st January 2015

I was 44 years old yesterday. We were due to go out tonight with a few friends to celebrate but Alison has been ill for a few days with sinusitis and isn't well enough so we have had to cancel. She is rarely ill and is more disappointed than me about missing a night out. I've had enough birthdays already to not worry about missing the celebrations for this one, it's not as though it is a special year.

This afternoon, I have had regular texts from Alan letting me know his thoughts about Ebbsfleet United, after he saw them draw 2-2 at Gosport Borough. His final text summarised things as follows :-

"Prepare for a draw mate (between North Ferriby & Ebbsfleet – Alan has already presumed Ebbsfleet will win their replay against Braintree). They play a similar style to Ferriby. They have a tall number ten, Adam Cunnington, who is the same as Tom Denton, but better on the floor. They also have the experienced Danny Kedwell, who holds the ball up well and he feeds off Cunnington. Sean Shields is an overlapping left back who sees a lot of the ball and their number eleven, Theo Lewis, is the playmaker in midfield. They play five at the back, but it moves to a three, to allow the wing backs to bomb on."

Alan may not have played football to a high level, but he has seen enough football over the years to understand the game, so I trust his judgement. That's both of us anticipating a trip to Kent for a replay now. Time will tell whether we are proved right. I will have a good laugh on Tuesday night if Braintree Town beat Ebbsfleet in their replay.

Tuesday 3rd February 2015

Luck has been on our side again. Ebbsfleet United's replay against Braintree Town was the only FA Trophy replay that took place tonight with the other two, Gateshead against Wrexham and FC Halifax Town against Dartford being victims of the weather once again. Perhaps Alan and I actually know more about football and fate than I give us credit for as Ebbsfleet United beat Braintree Town 2-0, which means it will be the Kent side who travel up to East Yorkshire on Saturday.

We are actually going to buck the trend of there being three of us at North Ferriby, as this time both my Dad and Jamie are coming with Alan and me. Some snow is set to hit the East Coast on Thursday and Friday, but if the forecasters are right, it is going to be milder on Saturday, so the game shouldn't be under threat.

The Quarter Final is going to be North Ferriby United's biggest test so far in the competition. Ebbsfleet United are no strangers to this stage of the FA Trophy. They actually won the competition in 2008, defeating Torquay United in front of a bumper crowd of 40 186 at Wembley.

The club only actually became Ebbsfleet United in May 2007, prior to that they were Gravesend & Northfleet. Going back to prior to World War Two, it was two separate teams, Gravesend United and Northfleet United.

In late 2007, Ebbsfleet United made national sporting headlines as they were taken over by the website 'MyFootballClub'. In a bizarre turn of events, a reported 27 000 members of the website all chipped in £35 each to, in effect, buy a say in team affairs at Ebbsfleet United. Each member had a say on team selection, transfers and any major event at Ebbsfleet was also put to a member vote. It was a novel idea, but the problem was that once the novelty wore off, the numbers of members who maintained an interest dwindled. Press interest led to a growth of members to around 32 000 but as time passed the numbers dropped off. By September 2010, the numbers had reportedly dropped to 3 500. In 2013, the members voted to pass two thirds of the shares to the supporters trust, 'Fleet Trust' and the other third to a major shareholder at the club. By May 2013, Ebbsfleet United were bought by a group of Kuwaiti investors who settled the financial problems that were troubling the club. With financial backing, an excellent season was anticipated in 2013-14 and a push for a Conference place was expected. Ebbsfleet United almost made it, only losing out to Dover Athletic in the play off final.

2014-15 has seen Ebbsfleet again in the top half of the Conference South but they will need a good finish to the season to gain another play off place, as they have been let down by their own inconsistency. A bad result tends to follow a good one, the perfect example was over the Christmas period. On Boxing Day they defeated one play off rival, Chelmsford City 5-1 and then on the 29th they lost 5-1 to another, Basingstoke Town. North Ferriby United will be hoping the latter Ebbsfleet United turn up at Grange Park (the EON Visual Media Stadium) on Saturday.

Thursday 5th February 2015

Having thought we would actually be taking four to North Ferriby on Saturday, it looks like we are now down to three. Jamie has phoned today to say he is struggling with an illness which he tried to avoid labelling 'man flu', but that appears to be what it is. He said the whole family have come down with it and he will be spending his weekend in a centrally heated house rather than at the side of a football pitch. Snow has started to arrive in East Yorkshire but there appears to be no signs of panic yet, as the forecast still remains that milder weather will arrive on Saturday.

Friday 6th February 2015

Once in a while I forget I am 44. Brad, my eldest son, plays for Croston Juniors Under 15s and they train on a Friday night on the excellent '4G' surface at the local school. I help the manager, John Harper, run the side and most Fridays, I like nothing better than to go in goal during the match we have at the end.

It was bitterly cold at training tonight, but that didn't bother me. I was having a fine old time in goal, commanding my area, making point blank saves and fooling myself into thinking I was 21 again. I came down to earth with a bump. One of the lads in the opposition side sprinted down their right wing, whipped in a near post cross and as I went to collect it, it was deflected off one of my defenders and headed towards the penalty spot, which was to my right. I twisted my left hip around, taking my body weight from my left ankle to my right, but with it being frosty and slippy underfoot (and with me weighing a portly 16 stone), my right ankle failed to tilt outwards and instead collapsed inwards. I felt an intense pain in my ankle, shouted (and according to Brad swore) and fell in a heap on the floor.

Fourteen and fifteen year old boys are not noted for their sympathetic nature so whilst I stayed down, they naturally laughed and continued. I could understand why they laughed but for me it wasn't a laughing matter. For the first 30 seconds, I thought I had broken my ankle, for the thirty seconds after that, as I hobbled off the pitch, I realised it was just a sprain, but the concern became a different one,

"How the hell am I going to get to North Ferriby tomorrow?"

It's a couple of hours later now and my ankle is twice its normal size but I managed to hobble to the car and most important of all, I managed to drive home without the pain being any worse. Touch wood, I should be OK. Maybe it's time I hung up my gloves completely but in all likelihood, once the sprain recovers, I will be back to leaping around like a madman once more.

Really looking forward to tomorrow's game now. Having been to thirteen of the fourteen FA Cup games with us last season, my Dad is joining us for the first time in the FA Trophy tomorrow, which will make it particularly special. I am picking Alan up from Buckshaw Parkway at twenty to eleven, so have told my Dad to get to our house for quarter to.

Tomorrow is North Ferriby's chance to put right the wrong from last season when they lost at home to Gosport Borough in the Quarter Final. A Semi Final place would put them in dreamland and if they win that, it could transform my book from a non-fictional football book into a fairytale.

Saturday 7th February 2015 – FA Trophy 4th Round

North Ferriby United v Ebbsfleet United

Attendance – 610

Today did not start well. My ankle continued to balloon and I struggled to sleep. At two o'clock, I made a hobbling attempt to get to the toilet and as I struggled through, Alison sat up in bed and said,

"You won't be going to the game tomorrow, Cal. I'll be taking you to the hospital for an X-Ray."

I felt sick, not because of the pain but because not making it to North Ferriby would ruin everything.

"I've got to go, Alison, Alan can't drive, it's not fair to ask my Dad and I can't write a book about an FA Trophy journey when I've missed two games."

"You haven't missed any other games."

"I did. When we were in Spain."

"Oh….. Calvin, it can't be helped. You might have fractured a bone in your foot."

"I'll be alright. It's painful but it's not agony. I'll be fine. Can you just nip down and get me some Ibuprofen and some paracetamol, hun? Thanks."

At that point, I was 90% sure everything was ruined. The pain was getting worse and I imagined by the morning it would be worse again. I wondered whether I could get Alison to nip me up to Chorley hospital in the early hours of the morning and get my Dad to drive us to Ferriby and I could go in on a pair of crutches. I was still convinced it was just a swollen ankle, but if I couldn't put my right foot on the ground, it was going to be difficult justifying a two hundred mile round trip for a football match.

"What about Joel's paper round?" Alison asked.

"I should be able to drive him around, he'll just have to put all the papers through," I said but I failed to convince myself, let alone Alison.

"I'll have to go with him if you can't walk."

I struggled to get to sleep thinking I'd have to ring Alan first thing and break the news. I thought about how Alan would have to write this Chapter and if there was a small fracture in my leg, how I would have to get to the rest of the games on crutches.

Alison also said she struggled to sleep. Her concerns were much more logical. If I had broken a bone and was on crutches, how was I going to be able to do my job? Would I get paid? How would we pay all the bills? Would we slide back into the financial mess we had just spent the last eighteen months crawling out of?

For once, the sporting (& financial) gods smiled on me. I went to sleep imaging the worst, but when my alarm went off at six fifteen, I noticed the pain had subsided a little and, even more importantly, I could put some weight, tentatively, on my right foot. Perhaps if I wasn't due to go to a football match, I would not have played it down, but if I could hobble, I was going.

"My foot's fine, Al," I announced triumphantly.

"It doesn't look fine."

"Well, maybe not fine, but a bit better. Definitely a bit better."

It's not fine. It still bloody sore, but I've got to East Yorkshire and back on it, so I'm positive it's nothing more than a sprain. Panic over.

By eleven o'clock this morning, my Dad and Alan were sat enjoying a cup of tea at our house and renewing old acquaintances. I had resisted the child like inclination to give Alan Joel's Manchester United mug but still received a telling off for forgetting how he took his tea,

"Bloody hell, Cal, I thought you would have known by now. No sugar, mate, no sugar. What's he like, Rich?" Alan asked in his sharp, Mancunian tones.

Without a stop at Jamie's for hot sausage rolls, we were at the ground and in the clubhouse for one o'clock. We had only met John Rudkin and his partner, Julie, once before at Farnborough, but we had traded so many messages with him over the last few months via social media, we greeted them like old friends. I had grabbed three pie and chips from the pitchside cabin and my Dad bought me a pint and soft drinks for the teetotal Alan and himself and we sat down with Alan and Julie to chew the fat.

I was interested to know a bit more about John. He is a youthful looking 53 and had played in goal until he reached fifty. In his prime, he had played for Winterton Rangers in the Northern Counties East Football League Division One. When he first began his association with North Ferriby United, three years ago, it was purely as a fan and he hasn't missed a game home or away since, but prior to the start of this season, Les Hare, the Chairman, asked John if he would take on the role of Social Media Manager. It has turned out to be perfect timing as John's dedication and enthusiasm for the role has co-incided with another excellent FA

Trophy run for the club. During the ninety minutes of the match, John also doubles up as a club photographer, along with David Gill.

"How many do you think will be here, today, John?" I queried.

"Over six hundred, I reckon. There's starting to be a fair bit more interest now but if we get through today, then the real interest will start then. I think if we get to the Final, if all the Hull City fans jump on board, we could take five thousand to Wembley."

Like us, John was beginning to dream of a North Ferriby United Wembley appearance. Ebbsfleet United shared that dream though and they had not come to East Yorkshire with anything other than a win in mind.

Ebbsfleet United had brought a couple of hundred friendly fans with them and most of them were trying to squeeze into the narrow clubhouse, so by two o'clock, Alan, my Dad and I decided to make some room and head out into the ground. Alan had a quick word with Billy Heath, the North Ferriby United manager to see if he needed a heads up on Ebbsfleet, but it turned out Ferriby had done their homework and were particularly aware of the attacking dangers of Danny Kedwell and Adam Cunnington.

My Dad's knees and back are showing signs of a sporting life, so we opted to take seats on the far side of the ground for once, rather than to stand on the terracing. Whilst there, my Dad took a call on his mobile from Wally Bennett, a close friend and former team mate from the 1967 FA Amateur Cup Final.

"I'm at a match with Calvin," my Dad explained.

"Which match?"

"North Ferriby United."

"Who?"

Remember the name, as Clive Tyldesley famously said about Wayne Rooney. If North Ferriby United win today, they will be taking another giant step in their campaign to become better known on the English footballing map.

Once both teams came out to warm up, at about quarter past two, I thought it was a good opportunity to quiz my Dad about his pre-match preparations. Back in the sixties, the players were only told to arrive at the ground at half past two, went out to warm up at five to three, with two balls per team, one for the attackers to kick amongst themselves and one for the defenders. Once in a while, someone would take a shot at the goalkeeper and balloon the ball into a neighbouring back garden. My Dad remembered one game when both balls went over the fence and the coach refused to give them any more so they had to do their few minutes warm up without any balls. How times have changed at top non-League level. Pre-kick off now, it's near enough one ball each.

We began to discuss the logistics of a replay on Tuesday in Kent and my Dad, purely on watching both sides extensive warm ups, decided it was unlikely there would be one.

"I hope I'm wrong, but just watching both sides warm up, it seems to me like Ebbsfleet United are going to win this easily. They control the ball better, shoot better and pass the ball around quicker. They look like much the stronger side."

Alan and I took it in turns to explain that the one thing that my Dad had not factored into his judgement was spirit. North Ferriby United were a spirited side.

They may not knock the ball around like South Americans but once the game started they would make things very difficult for Ebbsfleet United with their tenacious attitude.

As we were in the stand at the far end of the ground, the side of the pitch at the bottom of the slope, we noticed there was a fair bit of packed snow by the advertising boards. Les Hare the Chairman had organised an army of volunteers to come to the ground on Friday afternoon, to ensure the pitch was playable. It looked heavy down by the touchline but definitely fit for purpose.

Just prior to kick off, Trev Cunnington and his son-in-law, Phil Kirkham, arrived. It was Phil that introduced Trev to North Ferriby United, having lived in North Ferriby for a few years and also Phil who bought Trev my book for Christmas. We did the introductions, as they took the seats in front of us.

"I knew you were Alan," Phil said cheerily shaking Al's hand, "I recognised you from the back cover of the book."

Trev had brought the book back again, knowing my Dad was coming, to get him to sign it too. We need to get Phil Cooper and Jordan Oliver along to North Ferriby and then he would have the collection.

I know from last season that there is a tendency to write the script in your mind for these Cup competitions and then reality comes and tramples all over them. Last season, it was at this stage that Everton bowed out to Arsenal and spoilt my FA Cup dreams and as the game kicks off, Ebbsfleet immediately look like they have the potential of ending this season's dream of following one side through every one of their games to the final. Ebbsfleet are a big strong side who can more than match

North Ferriby for physicality. It's a pity Farnborough's manager, Spencer Day isn't here, as I could remind him that there are some 'brutal giants' in his own league. They can also play a bit too and Alan was right about the dangers of the strike force who seem to link up naturally. Adam Cunnington is a tall, mobile striker, good in the air and with the ball at his feet whilst Danny Kedwell is a solid unit, think of a Neil Ruddock frame, in condensed form, with a backside borrowed from Kim Kardashian.

North Ferriby United started brightly with Fry sending a free kick just wide but soon a sense of nervousness seemed to take hold. It was though fate was whispering the word 'Wembley' in their ears and unsettling them. Even the seemingly unflappable goalkeeper, Adam Nicklin, was displaying human characteristics for once and raced off his line one time too many, fuelled by adrenalin and miskicked a clearance that almost led to an Ebbsfleet goal.

Alan and I had raised Adam Nicklin's status to my Dad to almost Banks and Yashin proportions pre-match so Alan was keen to offer an explanation.

"Nerves must be getting to him, Rich, that's the first mistake we've seen Nicklin make in six games."

Billy Heath, the North Ferriby United manager, must have known Ebbsfleet tended to play a 3-5-2 formation, so had packed his own midfield too, playing 4-5-1 with Adam Bolder playing in the middle alongside Russell Fry and Liam King. This formation had worked well in the second half of the Farnborough game to nullify the chances of the opposition but with a congested midfield, it appeared very early into the game that it would be a match of very few chances.

As it turned out there were a number of half chances but very few clear cut ones. Jason St Juste was prospering from the gaps left in the Ebbsfleet defence by their full backs pushing up and he looked the main danger for North Ferriby. He appeared to have provided the pass for the opening goal, when he slipped an intricate ball through to Liam King, who had darted forward and beat the Ebbsfleet keeper Preston Edwards with a neat lob, only to discover he had been flagged offside. I jumped out my seat to complain only to discover there were very few other dissenting voices either on the pitch or off it.

Around thirty minutes into the half, Ebbsfleet United looked to have taken the lead as Kelvin Langmead, the former Shrewsbury Town, Peterborough United and Northampton Town defender had a header that looked destined for the bottom corner, but frustratingly for the healthy away support, they saw the ball rebound to safety after hitting the base of the post. After that let off, North Ferriby seemed to raise their game and the central midfield trio of Bolder, Fry and King began to dictate proceedings.

This was also the first chance we had to cast our eyes and make a judgement on Sam Topliss, who had joined on loan from Hull City. Topliss is a right back who has played regularly for the Hull City U21's side for a couple of seasons without forcing his way into the first team squad. Our initial impression was that he looked very accomplished, was quick, had good control, defended adeptly and liked to get forward along the right wing.

Topliss also seemed to be forging a good understanding with Danny Clarke, the North Ferriby midfielder. Clarke is not pretty on the eye in a footballing sense. He has an awkward run with his shoulders tucked into the base of his head, but would probably be a dream client for ProZone statisticians as he does not stop running throughout the ninety minutes. He was also looking a lot more dangerous up the right wing than he had at Farnborough, with his control much better and he even went close to scoring with a spectacular overhead kick that went narrowly over. Clarke played at Ferriby for two seasons from 2012 but left due to work commitments and had been plying his footballing trade recently for Hull United, five tiers lower in the pyramid until rejoining in January. Clarke is definitely one of the unsung heroes of the Ferriby side, not attracting the same attention as the likes of Nicklin, King, Denton and St Juste, but definitely a player who adds significant value.

Down the left wing, Jason St Juste, the pacier, more flamboyant wide man continued to create chaos in the Ebbsfleet ranks and he had a powerful shot beaten away by Preston Edwards. Soon after this, Anthony Acheampong, the tall, muscular Ebbsfleet defender, formerly at Barnet, suffered a head injury in a collision and had to be substituted. He was clearly concussed as the tannoy announcer asked if there was a Doctor in the stadium and as a precaution an ambulance was called for. It was a sad end to a tense, exciting first half which finished goalless. Our five judges, Alan, my Dad, Trev, Phil and myself had it about level on points. Discussions about Tuesday night trips to Kent were beginning in earnest.

As we headed around the ground at half-time to grab a cup of tea, we had a quick chat with John Rudkin, who was once again taking photos pitch side. The photos of the Ferriby games by John and club photographer, David Gill, are always excellent and help capture the drama of the day. John is feeling a little frustrated with the referee who he feels hasn't allowed the game to flow. The Ebbsfleet United fans who were near us, who came across as a friendly bunch and seemed to avoid the blatant bias of some supporters, had made similar comments. I understood the point, sometimes it would be great if the ref refrained from blowing his whistle for a moment or two, just to see if any advantage can be gained. No-one was saying he was a bad referee, just a bit whistle happy.

When the second half started, it was Ebbsfleet United who began the brighter. The pre-match superlatives that Alan and I had used to describe Adam Nicklin were vindicated when he made a string of top class saves to keep the game scoreless. The best save came after a Dean Pooley free kick was sliced towards the Ferriby goal by a defender and as it span and dropped towards what appeared to be an empty net, Nicklin arched his back, stretched out his arm and managed to claw the ball on to the post. A few minutes later he made a further fine save from another powerful Kevin Langmead header but even when Ebbsfleet managed to get past Nicklin, they found luck to be against them. One chance dropped invitingly to Adam Cunnington, on the half volley, just outside the box and he let fly with an absolute thunderbolt that hit the underside of the bar, dropped on to the goal line and then span away to safety. The venom Cunnington put into the shot drew gasps from both sets of supporters and minutes later the crossbar still seemed to be rattling.

Having ridden their luck for the first fifteen minutes of the second half, North Ferriby regained their composure and began to edge their way back into the game. One of the other unsung heroes from the North Ferriby United side, Russell Fry always seems to come into a game more as it progresses as he has bags of stamina. We only saw him start a game for the first time in the Boston United replay, but he is a battler who is also a wizard with a dead ball. When North Ferriby United had a free kick just outside the box, to the left of centre, it was Fry who stepped up with a curling, dipping right footed free kick, that was beating Preston Edwards to his right, but we watched despairingly as it struck the bar.

As players on both sides began to tire on a heavy pitch, Jason St Juste, with his trickery and pace, began to emerge as a threat once more. He went on one long run, leaving several Ebbsfleet players with the 'Wile E Coyote' blues as he sped past them like the Road Runner, possibly adding a 'Beep, Beep' as he flew by. St Juste put a perfect ball through to Liam King, who had sprinted forward to offer an option to his speedy team mate. Our hopes were raised as King raised his foot back but his well struck shot only found the side netting.

By now, Alan and I were convinced a replay was a certainty. Both keepers and both sets of woodwork, seemed unbeatable. The Ebbsfleet United fans behind us in the stand were telling us the best route to take and I was all set to book a half day off work. Then, out of nowhere, something crazy happened.

In the 86th minute, North Ferriby United had a corner. As the ball was swung in, there was the ubiquitous grappling that takes place at every corner at every game these days and then the predictable sound of the ref's whistle for a foul against a defender. This time though, I did a double take as the referee appeared to be pointing towards the penalty spot. Surely not? Maybe he was just pointing towards where he wanted the free kick to be taken from. Then, the Ferriby players started celebrating, the Ebbsfleet players started protesting, but not vigorously and a few seconds later, it became more obvious why, as Ross Joyce the referee brought Kenny Clark towards him and then showed him the red card.

"What did he do, Dad?" I asked puzzled.

"No idea, there's no-one on the floor and no-one clutching their face, did you see it Alan?"

"No, Rich."

In fact, no-one around us saw anything, but even the Ebbsfleet fans agreed Clark must have done something to be ordered off. Our focus slowly moved off the incident we had all obviously missed and moved on to the crucial penalty.

Alan and I always talk about game changing moments. This wasn't just a game changing moment. For me, this penalty was a tie changing moment. Not to put too fine a point on it, it was a life changing moment. If the penalty went in, Ferriby were solid and well organised enough to survive the few surviving minutes, they would be through to the Semi Finals for the first time in their history. If the keeper saved it or it was missed, Ferriby would be out. They may have gone to Boston United and won, but I didn't see lightning striking twice. Ebbsfleet United were by far the best team North Ferriby had come up against and this was Ferriby's moment to defeat them. Miss it and in my opinion, the dream of Wembley was over.

Liam King, North Ferriby United's youthful looking captain took the ball from the referee and placed the ball on the spot. Nathan Jarman, the club's usual penalty taker, who had scored from the spot three times in November, had been out the side recently and Ferriby hadn't been awarded a penalty since. Adam Bolder, the vastly experienced former professional had already been substituted so perhaps as captain, King was showing the leadership qualities that earned him that role. Score and Clark was going to be the villain of the piece, miss and Liam King and the rest of the North Ferriby United side would have been left with memories of what might have been.

It is hard to spot nerves from fifty metres away but Liam King didn't appear to be nervous. To Kent or not to Kent, that was the question. King took a fairly long run up, at pace and then expertly smashed the ball towards Preston Edwards right hand post. The keeper has played almost 200 games for Ebbsfleet and had looked accomplished all day, but the precision of the penalty left him helpless, it rolled inside the post. 1-0 to North Ferriby United! A jubilant King ran off to the corner to celebrate, ending up at the bottom of a player pile on.

"Fantastic! Watch this now, Rich, Ferriby will kill this game dead," Alan commented.

Each time we had seen North Ferriby United before, once they took the lead it had rarely been threatened, but the calibre of the opposition had not been to Ebbsfleet's standards. Boston United are a similar level but in the replay, they ran out of ideas. I expected Ebbsfleet to drum up one last opportunity or at least part of me did.

I tend to watch football matches these days with an angel of optimism and a devil of pessimism perched on my shoulders. The angel is telling me Alan is right, North Ferriby will tighten up, will be rock solid and they will be through to the Semi-Finals. In fact, the angel tells me, this is their year, they are going all the way to Wembley and you've bought that lucky ticket to witness history in the making. The devil, on the other shoulder, is telling me to get a grip, Ebbsfleet United will get that chance, score it, the traffic to Kent will be horrendous on Tuesday, Ebbsfleet will run riot in the replay, draw Dover Athletic in the Semi Final and we will have two further trips to Kent for the Semis and then a trip to Wembley to watch two teams we have no affiliation to.

In the last minute of injury time, fate decided to play with my emotions. Adam Cunnington laid the ball off to Danny Kedwell inside the Ferriby box. For once he had no North Ferriby United defenders snapping at his ankles like piranhas. Kedwell had time to pick his spot, but opted for power rather than precision. If the ball had nestled in the corner of the Ferriby net, Kedwell would have been carried off the Ferriby pitch by the jubilant Ebbsfleet travelling support, but instead it flew high over the bar and into the 5-a-side court behind the goal and the Kent supporters held their heads in their hands. For them, the dream of Wembley was over. Once Nicklin booted the retrieved ball into the Ebbsfleet United half, Ross Joyce sounded his whistle to signal an end to a dramatic match. Another Chapter of the 'Ferriby Fairytale' had been written and a happy ending was in sight.

Most of the Ebbsfleet United supporters in the stand took defeat well and wished the North Ferriby United fans well in the Semi Final. A small band of Kent supporters, mystified by the penalty decision, gathered by the entrance to the changing rooms to aim some verbal abuse at referee, Joyce.

"You don't know what you're doing! You don't know what you're doing!"

I can empathise with the reaction of the supporters. It is horrible to lose a game that you are desperate to win, but that miserable, energy sapping gloom feels so much worse when you feel like your team have been the victims of a glaring error.

It turns out rather than be ridiculed, Ross Joyce really should have been given a pat on the back, as he spotted an incident most supporters, from both sides, had failed to see. Jamie Day, the Ebbsfleet United manager, was candid enough to admit, in post match interviews, that he had asked Kenny Clark whether he had swung an elbow at Ferriby's centre back, Danny Hone and Clark had admitted that he had.

Fleet boss Day said: "I spoke to him after and he elbowed someone after the ball had gone and you can't do that. I'm disappointed with that because it's cost us a replay on Tuesday.

The performance was good, the way they battled and the effort they put in, there's nothing wrong with the performance. The disappointing thing was the way we've given the penalty away. We dealt with the cross in the first place and then to give it away, like we have done, off the ball, it's not acceptable.

That's the disappointing thing because they dug in for 90 minutes and Clarky's let the boys down and he's let the club down.

I couldn't see them scoring and I think it would have been a totally different game at our place, with our pitch being nice – I think it would have suited us. Discipline has cost us and that's not acceptable.

When it's in the 85th minute and he's played in a game that he knew was going to be physical, I can't understand why he's done it. I can't defend him because he's said he's clearly done it and that's not good enough. He's let everyone down at the club and we've told him that. I think we have to look into it because you can't be throwing elbows at people. If it was the other way round, we'd be going mad. I think there needs to be action taken because it's not good enough."

  I don't know Jamie Day, have never met him and do not know if he is a good man or a good manager, but when I read these comments, I felt a sense of admiration for him. In the Premier League these days, it is very, very rare for a manager to speak out against one of his own players. If a player dives, the manager insists there was a slight touch. If a player commits a red card offence, the manager will argue it should have been a yellow and will point out equally bad fouls from opposition players that did, in fact, warrant a red card. Everyone seems quick to provide an excuse but slow to take any responsibility for their team's actions. Referees have become scapegoats. No-one ever loses because they were the second best team in the game in the Premier League, they lose because they were somehow cheated. If Premier League supporters were polled on whether referees were the worst they have ever been, 95% would probably say they are. They aren't, they are just put under more pressure and scrutiny than ever before.

In an even game, Jamie Day didn't try and find an excuse. He didn't throw in the BUT word either. 'Clark did use his elbow BUT North Ferriby United did this or that'. There was none of that. Clark has let us all down, that was the message. He had too. He probably didn't need telling. Kenny Clark had a long coach trip back to Kent to reflect on the fact that Ebbsfleet United would not be walking out at Wembley on 29th March and in no small part, that was down to him.

Despite one player's momentary lapse of reason, I came away thinking a lot of good thoughts about Ebbsfleet United. They played good football, battled hard, had friendly, encouraging fans and an honest manager. I hope they get over their disappointment and finish their season on a high.

As for North Ferriby United, their sensational FA Trophy journey just kept rolling on. My Dad commented that he had seen far better non-League sides in his time, but Ferriby's spirit of togetherness, their battling qualities from front to back and the fact that they are a well organised side could even take them to Wembley. He was particularly impressed with Adam Nicklin in goal, Danny Hone at centre back and Jason St Juste on the left wing.

History had been made at North Ferriby United today. They were FA Trophy semi-finalists for the first time ever. As part-timers, they could easily now have to beat a professional side with full-time players to reach Wembley, as most Conference clubs had full-time playing staff. If they could get a Semi Final draw that took them away first and could hold out for a draw or a narrow defeat, it would be nerve jangling watching them in the second leg.

John Rudkin tweeted on the North Ferriby United twitter page tonight that if he sees any more of Alan and me, he is going to have to marry one of us! I replied that he can marry Alan and I will be 'Best Man'. We have now seen North Ferriby United six times in the FA Trophy and the two semi-finals will be games seven and eight. A ninth game at Wembley would truly put the icing on the cake.

FINAL SCORE :- North Ferriby United 1 Ebbsfleet United 0

Sunday 8th February 2015

If it is exciting for Alan and me to witness this fantastic cup run of North Ferriby United's, I can only imagine how exciting it is for the fans, players and officials of the club. The 2013-14 season had been their first in the Conference North and the doom mongers predictions of first season relegation proved unfounded as North Ferriby finished Runners Up. This season they have had another upper half season in Conference North with the FA Trophy campaign leading to more and more people discovering who North Ferriby United are and where they are located. If you are one of the two to three hundred regulars at North Ferriby, the last few seasons must have been incredible. Northern Premier League (Evo-Stik) Champions in 2012/13, Conference Runners Up in 2013/14 and at the very least FA Trophy Semi-Finalists in 2014-15. Billy Heath, the manager, and all the staff at North Ferriby have done an incredible job. A trip to Wembley would complete a sensation treble.

Last night, I received a tweet from Peter Wanless, the NSPCC Chief Executive, congratulating North Ferriby and saying how disappointed him and his son were that Ebbsfleet United had been knocked out. I hope my footballing travels lead me to meet up with Peter some time soon.

Other FA Trophy Results

Third Round Proper

FC Halifax Town 3 Dartford FC 1

Gateshead 2 Wrexham 2

(*After Extra Time. Wrexham won 5-3 on penalties).

Fourth Round Proper

Dover Athletic 3 Bath City 3

Torquay United 1 FC United of Manchester 0

Thus, so far, only North Ferriby United and Torquay United have made it through to the Semi Finals. FC Halifax Town have had real problems with their pitch so to ensure they could fulfil their Third Round Proper game, they switched the tie to Droylesden FC, which is spitting distance from the Etihad, Manchester City's ground, but over thirty miles from Halifax. They will have been pleased that 451 still turned up to cheer them on to victory and set up a Quarter Final tie with penalty kick victors, Wrexham.

Tomorrow, the FA Trophy Semi Final draw is being broadcast on Colin Murray's Talksport radio show. The teams that North Ferriby United could be drawn against are as follows :-

i) Torquay United.
ii) Bath City or Dover Athletic.

iii)   FC Halifax Town or Wrexham.

Four of these five clubs are in the Vanarama Conference, so it would be a tall order for North Ferriby to have to overcome them over two legs, but not impossible. I keep saying to Alan it'll be Torquay United, so we can visit my friend since schooldays, Andrew Berry but from a North Ferriby United perspective, the ideal scenario would be if Bath City defeated Dover Athletic in their replay and North Ferriby were drawn against them. Bath City are the other non-Conference team left, as they are in Conference South, but having already knocked out Bristol Rovers and Altrincham from the Conference and drawn away at Dover Athletic, they are going to be a very good side too. I would be delighted if North Ferriby United made it to Wembley, but my gut feeling for some time is that it will be a Torquay United – Wrexham final.

Monday 9th February 2015

When North Ferriby United's FA Trophy campaign began with a home tie against Mickleover Sports, I am sure Mark Carroll, the Ferriby Assistant Manager was not anticipating being the guest of honour on TalkSport for the live Semi Final draw. TalkSport seem to have reached an agreement with the FA to broadcast an early round of the FA Cup plus latter rounds of the Trophy & Vase. All three need the extra publicity so it is probably a good fit for all concerned.

With it being the FA Trophy Semi-Final draw, it was obviously not going to last very long, but, it transpired to be the best possible draw North Ferriby United could have hoped for. It was :-

Dover Athletic or Bath City v North Ferriby United.

Wrexham or FC Halifax Town v Torquay United.

As Colin Murray pointed out on his show, this was one draw that you did not want to be drawn out as the 'Home' team in, by being drawn out the hat first (or third). The 'Home' teams play their home leg first and the away leg second. It has always been thought that it is a slight advantage to play the home leg second. I am not sure if there is any statistical evidence to back this up, but North Ferriby United will at least have a slight psychological advantage.

The fact that potentially North Ferriby United could also play the other team who are not in the highest non-League tier (the Vanarama Conference) is also good news. If Bath City win their replay against Dover Athletic, it will be a Conference North team against a Conference South team. No matter who wins the Halifax-

Wrexham Quarter Final, the other Semi will be contested by two Vanarama Conference sides.

Whether it is Bath City or Dover Athletic, I have a feeling they may be victims of over confidence by concluding that they only have to get past little North Ferriby United to get to Wembley. It is a bit like the famous Milk advert of the early 1980's. For anyone below the age of 40, the advert had two Liverpudlian kids going into the kitchen for a drink after playing football. The conversation went something like this :-

Visiting Kid :- "Got any lemonade?"

Kid In Fridge Getting Out A Pint Of Milk :- "Might have."

Visiting Kid :- (seeing what his mate is pouring out) Milk?

Kid In Fridge :- Ian Rush drinks milk.

Visiting Kid :- Ian Rush?

Kid In Fridge :- Yeh & he says if you don't drink milk, you'll only be good enough to play for Accrington Stanley.

Visiting Kid :- Accrington Stanley! Who are they?

Kid In Fridge :- Exactly!

This advert was copied by millions of schoolkids up and down the country for years and gave Accrington Stanley the unwanted and incorrect reputation of being the team you played for if you were hopeless. I once did a presentation at Accrington

Stanley FC and joked that I had always wanted to play for them, ever since the day I was diagnosed as lactose intolerant. No-one laughed.

The relevance to North Ferriby United is that I could visualise the Bath City/Dover Athletic players saying before their Quarter Final replay,

"If we win tonight lads, we'll only have to beat North Ferriby United to get to Wembley."

"North Ferriby United! Who are they?"

"Exactly!"

I am probably doing the Bath City and Dover Athletic players a disservice by saying that, but it is only natural, at least to some extent, to presume North Ferriby United are an easier side to face than a Conference side. To prove my own point, I am already thinking Bath City would be an easier proposition for Ferriby than Dover Athletic.

The replay takes place at Bath City's Twerton Park tomorrow night and I have a couple of other reasons for wanting a Bath City victory other than it just potentially giving North Ferriby United a better opportunity of reaching Wembley. One is geographical and financial. In 'Another Saturday & Sweet FA', I was candid about my financial woes. I have avoided going down that route in this book as I am in a stronger financial position twelve months along the line, but money is still tight. Three football matches in February in the FA Trophy puts a bit of a strain on me and a trip to Dover from Chorley is always going to be more expensive than a trip to Bath. Also, Dover, as a Conference Club, probably charge a higher admission price.

A second reason is the potential of getting friends to attend a match at Bath is higher than getting friends at Dover. Having lived in Gloucestershire for over three years, there will hopefully be a few old friends who would meet up with us at Bath, as Gloucester is only 45 minutes away and some friends even live in the Bristol/Bath area. Having never lived in Kent, I doubt anyone would come to Dover.

Bath City will no doubt feel their name should already be in the hat without the addition of 'or Dover Athletic' alongside it. On Saturday, Bath City went 3-1 ahead in the 82nd minute at Dover and must have thought they were through, especially as Dover Athletic had had a man sent off. It wasn't to be though, as Dover fought back with an 87th minute goal to reduce the deficit to one and then a 94th minute equaliser. Alan thinks Bath City will win now they are at home, but I feel that Dover may grasp the lifeline they have been handed and show their Conference class in the replay. In 24 hours, we will see who was right.

Tuesday 10th February 2015

Alan was right and I have to say that I am very pleased that he was. Bath City defeated Dover Athletic 2-1 tonight and will now meet North Ferriby United over two legs on Saturday 21st February and Saturday 28th February. In the other Quarter Final played this evening, Wrexham won 1-0 away at FC Halifax Town and will meet Torquay United in the Semi Final. Bath City and Wrexham are at home first.

I forgot to mention yesterday, the fact that Torquay United and Wrexham have both been picked in the same side of the draw ensures that my prediction of a Torquay-Wrexham final will not be correct. It will be a Conference side against a side a tier below them, either a Conference North or South one. Alan and I are pretty desperate for North Ferriby United to get to Wembley now, it would be a bit of a hollow feeling seeing North Ferriby United eight times and then bow out and go to Wembley and see two teams play when you don't really care who triumphs. We want to be in the North Ferriby United end, watching players we have grown to know, with people we have got to know, that would just be fantastic and every time I think of it, I try to tell myself the more I want it, the less likely it is to happen. Superstition aside, after tonight, North Ferriby have a 50-50 chance of appearing at Wembley which is amazing.

The other thing I have thought about recently is how disappointed I would have been to miss out on the North Ferriby United cup run, if I had not taken up Alan's offer to do the FA Trophy this year and the FA Vase next. To an extent, I am unsure whether North Ferriby would have even had the Trophy run if we had not attended, as I do believe in the 'Butterfly Effect' whereby if any one fan, player, coach or official had done one thing differently the whole set of events could have turned out differently. I suppose it's that 'Sliding Doors' principle applied to football. I always find it strange when people say things like, "if we had scored those three chances, we'd have been three up, instead of it still being nil-nil", because if the first one had have gone in, the whole passage of play from there on in would have been completely different and the second and third chances would not have materialised.

With the first leg being at Bath City, I now need to contact a few people to see if we can swell our numbers for this game. My Dad mentioned he fancied a trip to Bath, as he has never been. My friend since schooldays, Andrew Moss, who is now my accountant too, lives in Cheltenham so he might come, as might my old next door neighbours in Gloucester, John and Mark Goodchild, as they are big football fans. Finally, an old work colleague and good friend from my days at Yorkshire Building Society, Ed Payne may join us too, as he lives in Bristol. Ed originally hails from Plymouth and is a big Argyle fan, one of a small band of 'Pilgrims' who were at the very famous game at Carlisle United on the last day of the season in May 1999, when Jimmy Glass, the Carlisle keeper scored in injury time to ensure Carlisle's League survival. I will get phoning around tomorrow but whatever happens, Alan and I will be there.

Back in the 1980's, Liverpool fans used to say that if Ian Rush scored they would never lose. In 2015, North Ferriby United fans might soon start saying if 'The Casual Hopper' and his lanky sidekick come to watch us, we are unbeatable.

Saturday 14th February 2015

Things are taking shape now for next Saturday's FA Trophy Semi Final first leg. With regards to our little gang of "speccies", Alan and I are going to be joined by my Dad, John Goodchild, Mark Goodchild, Ed Payne and his son, Harry. Andrew Moss hasn't taken up the offer to join us, he doesn't know too much about football, that's why he's a Liverpudlian! In all seriousness, Andrew manages his eldest son's team and one of his two boys probably has a match in the afternoon next Saturday. My Dad, Alan and I will call in at Andrew's and his wife Sarah's in Cheltenham on our way down, for a quick hello and a cup of tea.

Alan and I are also going to feature in the match programme. In one of many co-incidences that have happened during this FA Trophy trail, the Bath City programme editor, Mark Stillman, contacted me via Twitter to say that he has read 'Another Saturday & Sweet FA' and would I be happy to do a piece for the programme, as he is aware that Alan and myself are doing an FA Trophy journey this season? I was delighted to. Mark seems like a good, friendly guy, passionate about his club and very keen to make the Bath City programme an excellent, varied read every home game. He has fired a number of questions through to me about where we started, what the highlights have been and how I think the two legged Semi-Final will pan out. I tried to be diplomatic, as well as honest, so said that I had seen a lot of North Ferriby United and was only aware of Bath City's performances because of their giant killing of three Conference sides, but suspect it will be very tight. That is all true, the diplomatic bit was not going on to say that I hope North Ferriby United squeeze through and we get to see them a ninth time, at Wembley.

Mark has also asked if I could send him a few photos from the FA Trophy so it's lucky Gordon Johnson came with us to Farnborough, otherwise I wouldn't have had any. Having received the answers to my questions and the photographs, Mark has decided to extend our section in the programme to two pages. Hopefully it may lead one or two people to check out 'Another Saturday & Sweet FA' and even if it doesn't, the programme will be a nice keepsake for Alan and me. Mark not only puts together the programme but also is the tannoy announcer at the game, so I said if we get into the ground early enough, we will go over and say hello.

Friday 20th February 2015

I am all set for tomorrow and our journey down to Bath for the first leg of the Semi Final. A place at Wembley awaits for the victors of the two legged Semi Final and although it is not massively lucrative like the FA Cup, I am sure there will be no player, supporter or official at either club that does not want to get to Wembley. For most players, it will be a once in a lifetime opportunity. The only North Ferriby United player that I can think of that may have played at Wembley before is Adam Bolder, although with some of them playing at international level as schoolboys or in the Lower Leagues, someone else may have also appeared. I will check that out with John Rudkin.

Prior to the game, Alan and I are meeting up with a journalist from the Hull Daily Mail, Charlie Mullan, to do an article for the paper about our FA Trophy adventure. The meeting was set up by John Colley, the North Ferriby United fan who has done everything he can to help promote my books since he read 'Another Saturday & Sweet FA'. I hope I get to meet him at some point to thank him for his endeavours.

My Dad is going to meet me in the morning at eight in Wigan, leaving his car there, as he did for some of our trips down South last season and then we are picking Alan up at Crewe train station around nine. Hopefully that should get us down to Cheltenham for a quick cup of tea with Andrew and Sarah Moss at about half ten and then it's less than an hour from there to Bath. Really looking forward to it and I'm hoping we journey home tomorrow night with North Ferriby United still in with a realistic chance of reaching the Final.

Saturday 21st February 2015 – FA Trophy Semi Final (First Leg)

Bath City v North Ferriby United

Attendance – 1 730

Other than the abandoned game due to fog at Mickleover Sports and my sprained ankle prior to the Ebbsfleet United game at North Ferriby, most things during this FA Trophy trail have gone to plan. For an hour this morning, I began to worry that everything was unravelling around me and I would be lucky to get to the game at all.

The day began fairly matter of factly. It was a cold, grey morning when I helped my youngest son with his paper round and when I arrived home, there was a missed call and a voicemail message from my Dad. Disappointingly, my Dad's message said my Mum had been unwell overnight, nothing serious but he wouldn't be able to come down to Bath with us. Having really enjoyed my Dad's company at the Ebbsfleet game, it was a shame that he could not come to Bath but totally understood that he needed to stay with my Mum if she wasn't well.

As I wasn't having to meet up with my Dad in Wigan, I decided to leave home about fifteen minutes later and it was during those fifteen minutes that it started to snow. It had been frosty overnight and the cloud cover had only kicked in around seven, so icy roads with a covering of snow on top made for hazardous driving conditions. Once I joined the M6, it was madness. Despite it snowing and despite there being warnings everywhere that there was an accident ahead, people were not slowing down nor leaving enough space between them and the car in front. I witnessed two minor shunts and saw the after effects of several others on both sides of the road. Two cars heading North had hit the central reservation in separate incidents, as they were probably too busy rubber necking the carnage on our side of the road to spot the dangers on their own side. After three minutes of progressing through the chaos, I came to a total standstill, as what I guessed was the most serious accident was still ahead. Forty five minutes later, I was about fifty metres further forward.

It was still only 8:45am, but I was due to pick Alan up at nine at Crewe train station and I was still stuck near Charnock Richard service station between Preston and Wigan, forty miles or so from Crewe. I gave Alan a ring to say I was going to be late getting him but at this stage, had no idea how late. Alan just said to keep him in the loop, as if I was going to be stuck for hours, he would just jump on a train to Birmingham and then pick one up to Bath. I also rang Andrew Moss to say I was stuck in traffic pandemonium on the M6 because half an inch of snow had come down, so I was going to abandon plans to stop at theirs and just head straight down to Bath. Andrew was fine about it, but his wife Sarah shouted through and asked whether this would mean their opportunity to get a brief mention in my book had now been lost!

During last year's FA Cup trail, Alan had christened me 'The Risk Assessor' as I was always weighing up the scenarios prior to them actually happening or, I guess, prematurely panicking. This was the case again this morning, as ten minutes after my phone call to Andrew the traffic started moving. A mile further along, there were three or four cars on the hard shoulder surrounded by police cars and ambulances with a couple of the cars, fine looking cars too, an Audi and Mercedes, written off.

I managed to pick Alan up about three quarters of an hour later than originally intended, by which time the dodgy weather had passed and the sun was out. Like me, Alan was disappointed that my Dad couldn't make it, but was still really looking forward to the day. The trip to Wembley on 29th March would be so much better if it was North Ferriby United that made it through and Alan was cautiously optimistic that they would do it. Bath City had managed to rest most of their side and still thump Farnborough 7-4 in midweek, but Alan felt if North Ferriby could get through today's game with a draw or a one-goal defeat, Bath City would struggle up at Ferriby.

When my Dad was planning to come with us, I was planning to park up in Bath city centre and do an hour or two of sightseeing with him, but once he cancelled, the sightseeing tour fell by the wayside too. When I lived in Gloucestershire, I used to go to Bath every Wednesday, as I had an arrangement with a large mortgage brokers called London & Country, to spend my Wednesday mornings there and Alan was willing to forego a trip around Bath, as he was keen to get to the ground, so our sightseeing in Bath today was restricted to McDonald's, William Hill's (for the token losing football accumulator), a Co-operative supermarket and a local bakery shop. We were in Charlie's bar, the bar next to Bath City's Twerton Park ground by half past one.

We had a busy 90 minutes before kick off. First of all, Alan and I bought three programmes, the extra one for Gordon Johnson, who had put a request in via Facebook. Mark Stillman does an excellent job with the programme and the two page article he had put together about our FA Trophy journey was great, he had even managed to cram five of the photos I had sent him in. We bought a drink from the bar, picked a table and no sooner had we sat down, we spotted John Rudkin and Julie come in.

"JOHN! JOHN! Over here, mate!"

Alan shouted over with his usual strong Mancunian tones. It must have confused the locals as a couple of dozen heads turned, probably wondering why a man from a city that had two of the Premier League's top sides was at an FA Trophy Semi-Final seemingly supporting North Ferriby United. John and Julie came over to join us along with the brother of North Ferriby's Chairman, Les Hare and his wife. We were sat amongst a couple of tables of North Ferriby fans and one guy who seemed particularly excited was a guy called Chris Holbrough, a member of the North Ferriby United management committee.

Chris is a really friendly guy. He looks a similar age to me, but is a North Ferriby lad and it must be an amazing feeling to see your local village side go on this incredible Cup run that takes them within touching distance of Wembley. I can empathise, thinking back to the Burscough FA Trophy heroics in 2003, but back then, the Final was at Villa Park due to Wembley being re-built so this would be even more special. It would also be a case of lightning striking twice for the lifelong North Ferriby fans as they had been to the old 'Twin Towers' Wembley Stadium when they lost the FA Vase Final in 1997, 3-0 to Whitby Town. I heard someone saying over a pint that North Ferriby United would be the first side to have played at the old and new Wembley's. I was going to point out that this wasn't true as loads of teams had, Everton, Liverpool, Manchester United, Manchester City and Arsenal all immediately sprang to mind, but perhaps he meant in non-League circles and anyway, no one likes a smart arse so I kept my mouth shut.

I also asked John Rudkin if any of the North Ferriby lads had played at Wembley before. John informed me that Adam Bolder had. Back in 2009, when

Bolder was at Milwall, they reached the League One Play Off finals against Scunthorpe United. Almost 60 000 watched a five goal thriller, but Bolder was on the wrong side of a 3-2 defeat. So, neither North Ferriby United the team or any of its players had ever tasted Wembley victory. Today, they had a great chance of making a giant stride towards that ultimate goal.

I text Ed Payne, Mark Goodchild and Charlie Mullan from the Hull Daily Mail, to let them all know that we were in the bar and soon after Charlie arrived with a photographer in tow. Charlie is an amiable Northern Irishman and after the introductions, he did a quick interview with Alan and me, before getting the photographer to take a few photos of us amongst the Ferriby fans. Apparently the article will be in the Hull Daily Mail one day next week, so I will have to get Jamie to grab us a couple of copies.

Soon after the photos, Mark and John Goodchild arrived and minutes later, Ed Payne and his son, Harry came through too. It has been a long time since I have seen John and Mark. Alison and I left Gloucester in late 2001 and I have seen Mark once since, when he went up to see Spurs play at Bolton Wanderers in 2002 or 2003, but haven't seen John since. They both look really well, especially John who is 65 now. He is not long back from representing Hampshire Over 60s cricket side in South Africa and looks like he has retained some of his tan.

John was always one to tell a good story and he told me another cracker today. John and his wife, Ann, left Gloucester not long after we did and ended up living in Christchurch, Dorset on the South coast. Recently Ann was out for the day with one of her friends and her boyfriend and came back home to tell John that her friends boyfriend was a former footballer but she wasn't sure who he was.

"Who did he play for?" John asked.

"I remember he said he played for Middlesbrough, Everton, Newcastle and Spurs. Can you think of anyone who played for them?"

"How old is he?" John enquired.

"Mid to late forties."

"Well, I can only think of one."

"Who?"

"Gazza! Paul Gascoigne!"

"That's him."

He said Ann was totally nonplussed about meeting one of England's most iconic footballers, probably because she's a Sunderland fan. John suggested he should take a few beers and a fishing rod and go and meet up with him, but I think the relationship finished before he ever got the opportunity.

Charlie's bar was jam packed by half two, so we left and entered the ground. As we entered, Alan said it reminded him of York Street, Boston United's ground and I knew what he meant. It was again like Emmett "Doc" Brown from Back to The Future had crammed us all in his DeLorean and taken us back to the mid-1950s. The dilapidated terraces behind the goals and the long, roofed terrace that ran along one side of the pitch reminded me of both Boston United and Workington. There is both a sadness and something that warms the cockles of your heart when you witness these once fine old stadiums. Both Mark and John Goodchild commented on the fact they had played there in days of old, John on several occasions. Like me, John was a goalkeeper, although he also made a decent centre forward. When I lived in Gloucester, he would occasionally turn out for our Sunday side when we were short of players. I remember him coming on as a substitute and scoring once when he was about 50. Sir Stanley Matthews would have been proud of him.

North Ferriby United were warming up at the end nearest the entrance, so we stayed to watch them, with me pointing out to Mark and John who each player was and what position they played in. Tom Nicholson was in goal for a shoot in and the reserve keeper was not having a 'going day' with every shot finding its way into the goal, even one that hit the post cannoned back into him and ended up in the back of the net. He seems a good guy to have around the squad though, cheerful and up tempo, he could even laugh at his own misfortune.

Watching North Ferriby warm up, they always look awkward and unimpressive. Tom Denton isn't going to grab you too many twenty yard strikes, so watching his gangly frame running up to shoot from the edge of the box is always uncomfortable. They look, at first glance, like a Sunday league side, but once three o'clock is reached and the ref blows his whistle, they seem to metamorphosize into this impenetrable force. I keep thinking one day it won't happen and they'll be like Cinderella without her red shoes or Samson without his long hair and the magic will fail to kick in. I hoped that today would not be that unfortunate day.

Prior to kick off, I had a chat with Ed and Harry Payne. Harry is only eleven and at this stage seems much quieter than his ebullient father. Ed tells me that Harry is a really good footballer and enjoys watching too and has already been taken to several Plymouth Argyle games. This lead on to Ed recounting the Jimmy Glass story when Carlisle United retained their League status after their on loan goalkeeper scored a last minute winner to defeat Plymouth. Ed was working up in Edinburgh at the time, so had ventured down to Carlisle and said he had never witnessed before or since the feeling that he was going to get his teeth kicked in one minute and then he was going to be hugged to death by a mass of grown men the next.

Alan is a natural mixer, especially amongst football fans, so whilst I was chatting to Ed and Harry, Alan was chatting to Mark and John. Bath City's mascot is a large pink pig, so when it appeared behind the goal, egged on by Mark and John, Alan went over to have his photo taken. He immediately posted the photo of himself with his arm around the mascot on social media which meant he set himself up for a load of lighthearted abuse from his mates back home, as well as from the terraces.

"Bet you've had your arms around some pigs in your time," was the best terrace shout.

"Not for a long while," Alan answered back.

Prior to kick off the two teams swopped ends, but we confidently decided to stay behind the goal that North Ferriby United would be kicking towards. Amongst the Bath City fans there were a few comments that it was slightly surprising that manager Lee Howells had left Nick McCootie on the bench after he had reminded the boss of his goalscoring threat with four goals in the victory over Farnborough.

The game started tamely. We were expecting Bath City to come out with all guns blazing and to pepper the North Ferriby United goal from the start, but this didn't happen at all, as both sides struggled to string a few passes together.

"Poor game, so far," I said to Alan after an uneventful first ten minutes had passed.

"It'll suit Ferriby, that," Alan commented.

A nil-nil draw would be good for Ferriby, but to an extent, I felt like the host of a party and Ed, Harry, John and Mark were my guests, so I wanted them to go home having had a great day out, so I was particularly keen for it to be a decent game. None of them would have been there if I hadn't told them I was going and John had driven a couple of hours up from the South coast, so I didn't want them heading home wondering why they had bothered. I needn't have worried. By the time ninety minutes had passed there was plenty for them to go home talking about.

Billy Heath, the Ferriby manager, had again gone for the same 4-5-1 formation that he had deployed against Ebbsfleet United, flooding the central midfield area and allowing Danny Clarke and Jason St Juste to push forwards to support big Tom Denton. The only change to personnel was Mark Gray coming in at centre back to replace the injured Gregg Anderson. Gray had played much of the Quarter Final too after Anderson had to be substituted with a shoulder injury after 14 minutes.

The first chance of note arose in the 15th minute when Bath's Chas Hemmings was harshly adjudged to have fouled Tom Denton and referee James Linington gave a free kick in a central position, five yards or so outside the box. Russell Fry is normally very accurate with his free kicks and I was anticipating Bath City keeper, Jason Mellor, having to be at his best, but unfortunately Fry's free kick drifted narrowly wide.

Chances remained at a premium, but the ball was more regularly down at Jason Mellor's end, in the Bath City goal, than it was at Adam Nicklin's for North Ferriby United. After 23 minues, Bath City conjured up their first real opportunity and it was a golden one too. A Bath City corner by Frankie Artus was cleared as far as

Chas Hemmings, who curled a ball back into the box. Bath City forward, David Pratt, looked sure to break the deadlock as he rose to head it from six yards out, but to the home fans frustration, he put the chance wide.

North Ferriby United were soon to punish Bath for failing to take their rare chance. Jason St Juste was released on the left, after a cross from the right was touched on in the air by Adam Bolder. St Juste, who within the last year has become a Saint Kitts & Nevis international, was able to embark upon one of his trademark mazy runs, beating Sekani Simpson and firing in a low cross back towards Adam Bolder. Bolder failed to get his toe to the cross, but as he had got in front of his marker, Dan Ball, he left the Bath City defender unsighted and Ball was helpless as the ball struck him and bobbled into the back of the net. 1-0 to North Ferriby United!

As Jason St Juste and several of the Ferriby players were mobbed by a handful of delighted Ferriby fans behind the goal, Alan and I exchanged contented looks. It was only twenty five minutes in to a three hour battle, but it was the dream start and it felt like a giant step towards Wembley for North Ferriby. In the FA Trophy there are no scenarios were away goals count double, but it at least meant that Bath City would have to score two to win the home tie and against a defence as mean as North Ferriby's and with a keeper as good as Adam Nicklin, that would be no easy task.

The rest of the half passed without incident. North Ferriby's midfield seemed to be nullifying the threat posed by Bath City and as a result the crowd of over 1700 were subdued. At half time, we decided to go around to the away end and once again watch the half from the end that North Ferriby would be attacking. The majority of the North Ferriby United fans, probably around one hundred in total, had gathered behind the goal we headed towards.

"I've been very disappointed with Bath City so far, they are one step from Wembley, you would think they would really be going for it and getting the big crowd behind them, but it just hasn't happened," John Goodchild commented, as we headed around.

I had expected Mark and John to have supported Bath City for this game. Mark still lives locally and although John doesn't, he spent a lot of his life in the South West and I had assumed that they would be cheering Bath on. As it turned out, they weren't really bothered either way and given we were in the North Ferriby end for the second half, they were quite happy to lend Ferriby their support. Mark even said whichever side reached the Final, they would come along to cheer them on.

Ed Payne, on the other hand, said on the way to the game, his son Harry had asked him who he would be supporting and he had said he was a neutral, but although originally from Devon, Ed said the last twenty years or so in the Bristol area meant he found himself leaning towards Bath. I couldn't blame him. I noticed a few years ago when I went to watch Skelmersdale United against Chorley with my Dad, I found myself cheering Chorley on, despite my Dad's links to 'Skem' and having spent my childhood living much closer to Skem than to Chorley. Ed said if Bath City made it to Wembley, he would come along, but if it was North Ferriby United, he would give it a miss.

Even though we were only a quarter of the way through the Semi Final, at half time I found myself only thinking positive thoughts on Ferriby's behalf. Adam Nicklin had been redundant in the Ferriby goal, the Peat-King-Bolder central midfield trio were all experienced heads and would continue not to give Bath City an inch and the more I thought about it, the more I thought the game and the tie were already tipped heavily in Ferriby's favour. They might not quite have one foot on the Wembley turf, but at this stage they felt close enough to be able to smell the grass.

Nothing at the start of the second half, convinced me that my half time analysis was going to be proved wrong, as the second half started how the first had played out, with very little happening and a disappointed home crowd thinking their team had failed to reach the heights they had reached in their all conquering Trophy run.

In the away end, the North Ferriby United fans, buoyed by the positive score on the pitch, were in excellent spirits, despite rain starting to fall on them in an uncovered terrace. Five of the younger travelling Ferriby fans decided they would make it their mission to try to distract the home goalkeeper, Jason Mellor, so went to stand directly behind the goal and for the whole forty five minute second half attempted to engage in conversation with the keeper. They kept repeating his name in various tones from very high to very low.

"Jason, Jason, Jason....poor kick, Jason...you should have come out for that one, Jason, do you not normally play in goal?"

To his credit, Jason Mellor was unperturbed and acted as though he was oblivious to their shenanigans. Ferriby midfielder, Danny Clarke, was put through on goal, but Mellor raced off his line to collect the ball bravely at Clarke's feet .

Bath City were very much on the back foot and North Ferriby forced a series of corners. Russell Fry is always dangerous from set pieces and twice he managed to find the head of centre forward, Tom Denton, but the big number nine was unable to direct his headers downwards and they went harmlessly over the bar.

Ten minutes into the second half, Denton won a header that fell to Adam Bolder, who put an equisite ball through between the Bath City centre backs, for the rapid Jason St Juste to sprint on to. One of the Bath City defenders attempted to head the ball back to Mellor in goal, but St Juste seized his opportunity and sped between defender and keeper, prodding the ball past Mellor in to the net. 2-0 to North Ferriby United and the Ferriby crowd behind the goal went wild. St Juste ran jubilantly to the corner flag and rather than punching it in a Tim Cahill like manner, turned and stretched his arms out, looking half like Andrew Flintoff in the 2005 Ashes series and half like Kate Winslet in Titanic. In this instance, Danny Clarke rushed to claim the part of Leonardo Dicaprio, but several other players soon joined in.

I started to think dangerous footballing thoughts. We were only 55 minutes into a three hour encounter, but surely this meant North Ferriby United would be shocking the non-League footballing community and heading to Wembley. This was surreal. Two-nil up in the away leg and Bath had barely mustered a shot on goal. If North Ferriby could continue in a similar manner and close this game out, there would no way on earth that Bath City would go back to East Riding and win by three. Alan and I, along with all the Ferriby fans around us, were desperate to see North Ferriby United complete the journey with an appearance in North London and it now looked for all the world that it was going to happen. I was in a state of delirious shock.

When I was eleven, I remember playing a cricket match at Hutton Grammar School on the outskirts of Preston and when we were getting smashed out of sight by a much better side and about to fall to a heavy defeat, a rather posh young boy who had come along to cheer on his friends, warned the home players,

"Don't count your chickens before they flutter!"

A few minutes after mentally beginning to plan my trip to Wembley in the North Ferriby United end, that posh little boy's well spoken, high pitched warning, came back into my head.

At half time, Bath City had brought on Nick McCootie to form part of a three pronged Bath City attack. The tactical switch initially seemed to allow the Ferriby midfield to boss proceedings, but as they tired after an hour of hard work on a heavy pitch, the Bath City forward line began to work their way into the game, as they were being fed more balls from a younger midfield. David Pratt was playing as the central man of the three and when a ball was played into the box to him, from the right of midfield, Pratt attempted to latch on to it. It was an innocuous ball through and was heading off towards the goal line, half way between the goal and the corner flag, but Pratt must have felt central defender, Mark Gray breathing down his neck and when he was given a slight shove from the side, Pratt went down theatrically. It was by no means a dive, as there was contact and Pratt was moving at pace, but it was a minor infringement at worst, however, referee James Linington pointed to the spot. Technically it was the correct decision, but as they are seldom given, the North Ferriby United players and bench felt aggrieved.

As previously mentioned, Alan and I often talk about game changing moments. The penalty was potentially not only a game changing decision, it was a tie changing decision, as all the momentum had been going North Ferriby's way and if the penalty was converted, Bath City were suddenly back in it. David Pratt picked himself up off the floor, grabbed the ball and placed it on the penalty spot to take the penalty himself.

Mark and John Goodchild were standing next to me. I had mentioned to them how highly I rated Adam Nicklin and having already made one vital penalty save against Boston United, they wondered whether I had confidence that he would save this one too. In a scene reminiscent of Brian Moore famously asking Kevin Keegan whether David Batty would score in the 1998 World Cup penalty shootout for England against Argentina (Keegan said "Yes", the correct answer was "No"), I tried my best to be Kevin Keegan.

As David Pratt raced up to take his penalty, Mark Goodchild asked,

"Will he save it?"

"No," I answered.

I wanted to be Kevin Keegan. I wanted to give the wrong answer and for Nicklin to save spectacularly like he had against Boston. I felt if Pratt didn't score, there would definitely be no way back, but he blasted his penalty high and just slightly to Nicklin's right. Nicklin had dived low and the ball sped over him and into the back of the net. 2-1 and Bath were right back in it.

The optimism I had had after St Juste's goal immediately evaporated and despite still leading away from home, I now became a doom merchant, as pessimism took over. For the first time in the game, both the Bath City players and their supporters were given something to cheer about and lift their spirits.

"They've blown it now, Al, Bath will keep pushing forward now. There's half an hour left including injury time. They need to cling on for dear life."

A lot of football is played in the mind as well as on the pitch. Once Bath City scored they transformed into a different side. Confident, aggressive, attacking and dangerous were not words that would have described them in the first hour, but that was what they became in the last thirty minutes. Bath City became the side I feared they would be from the first minute. I started to worry that our FA Trophy story would become like our FA Cup one. A fairytale ending ruined by other clubs who had forgotten to read the script.

Adam Nicklin had enjoyed a quiet afternoon but now had to show the form that had led me to conclude that he was the best keeper I had ever seen at below Conference level. Firstly, he saved from a Nick McCootie header after a fine cross from Andy Watkins. Billy Heath, Ferriby's manager, then took Adam Bolder off, bringing on Jonathan D'Laryea to try to bring fresh legs to midfield. Bolder had been playing furthest forward of the three central midfielders, but it was immediately clear that D'Laryea had been asked to sit deeper and help out the Ferriby defenders.

Nick McCootie was looking particularly dangerous and the big, muscular forward was a constant threat to the North Ferriby United defence. He had a second chance to score when a ball dropped to him on the edge of the box, but he powered his shot straight at Nicklin. Worryingly, Nicklin stayed down with what looked like a twisted ankle.

I remembered the pre-match warm-up and my thoughts that Ferriby's reserve keeper, Tom Nicholson was not having a 'going day'. To be signed for a Conference North side, Nicholson is obviously a decent keeper. The programme notes revealed he had played twice for England schoolboys so must be no mug, but a lot of goalkeeping is about confidence and if it doesn't feel quite right one day, it can play on your mind. To have to come into a game cold when your goal is being peppered is not ideal and I was anxious to see Nicklin get back to his feet. Nicklin was eventually helped up and evidently in some discomfort tried to soldier on, with his defenders helping him out with ground kicking duties from goal kicks. My concerns became longer term, even if he managed to get through the game, would he be fit for the second leg?

North Ferriby United were defending doggedly. Mark Gray had put the penalty incident behind him and was looking solid, with Danny Hone again impressing, along with full backs Sam Topliss and Josh Wilde. Tom Denton was also dropping deep to help out with defensive duties, especially with set pieces. At 44 and sixteen stone, I reckon I could still beat Denton in a sprint so St Juste is better to have up front to chase down when the ball is cleared. Billy Heath knows how to play to Denton's strengths though and if he is not ideal for the escape ball, he is ideal to help protect a lead when a rear guard action is required. To count up the amount of aerial balls he wins both offensively and defensively during the course of a game would require a calculator rather than an abacus.

Weathering a storm had become a forte of Ferriby's in their Trophy run, as they had emerged from 'backs to the wall' tests against Boston United, Farnborough, in the first half hour, and also even spells during the Ebbsfleet United game. They looked like they would emerge with a narrow victory at Twerton Park too, until the 85th minute, when Bath City left back and club captain, Andy Gallinagh, from midway inside his own half, struck a long, channel ball forward that was between Ferriby's right back Sam Topliss and the right sided central defender, Danny Hone. Hone has been a vital cog in the Ferriby wheel throughout the Trophy campaign but on this occasion, he gave Nick McCootie a yard head start, perhaps anticipating that Topliss would be able to track across to head the ball clear. Instead, the ball bounced twice between the two defenders and as McCootie raced forward, the ball sat ideally for him and he showed great technique in getting his right boot under the ball, sending a looping 25 yard strike directly over the despairing head of Adam Nicklin. Often those sort of shots fail to dip in time, but McCootie had caught this one to perfection and it dipped in, just under the bar. It was a beautiful strike, the best we had seen throughout the FA Trophy, but our loyalties were firmly with North Ferriby United now, so we could not enjoy it one bit.

Alan began to curse through sheer frustration and mindful of the fact that we had an eleven year old boy with us, I told him to tone it down, which he did immediately. We know each other well enough to hand out a bit of guidance from time to time. I occasionally tell Alan to watch his language and he often tells me to smarten my act up and have a shave.

I understood Al's frustration. We had lived through every second of the Ferriby fairytale and although we weren't locals, we were always made to feel part of the club. Their heartbreak was ours too. We recognised every player and had formed our own opinions of their strengths and weaknesses. To steal a footballing analogy from Howard Kendall, Alan was married to Manchester City, as I was to Everton, but we were both enjoying a passionate affair with North Ferriby United and did not want it to end. The players needed to dig deep now and ensure the fairytale did not became a horror movie and allow a 2-0 lead to become a 3-2 defeat.

The last ten minutes, including injury time, dragged horribly. We were cold, we were wet and we were a little fed up, but the last thing we wanted now was another goal. Ferriby had all eleven men behind the ball and just wanted to return to East Riding with the tie finely balanced at 2-2.

Ben Adelsbury, Bath City's substitute midfielder, was one of several players on the pitch who had experience of playing in front of bigger crowds than today's. He had previously made a couple of League Cup appearances for Swansea City and had been part of the Salisbury City team that made it all the way to the Third Round of the FA Cup, before bowing out 3-1 at Sheffield United's Bramall Lane, in front of a crowd over 10 000. Adelsbury had come on after 69 minutes and played well enough to give Lee Howells, the Bath City head coach, a selection headache for the second leg. In the final few minutes, he had a well struck shot well saved by Nicklin, then sent a cross into the six yard box, which was pleading for a forward to capitalise on, but Ferriby captain, Liam King managed to track back and head over his own bar. Thankfully, that was the last of the goalmouth action and after everything looking so positive when Jason St Juste scored the second Ferriby goal, the feeling amongst the North Ferriby United fans was that a draw was a fair and potentially a positive result.

Alan and I said our farewells to Ed and Harry Payne, as well as John and Mark Goodchild. The Paynes said they would see us at Wembley if Bath City made it through, the Goodchilds said they would see us there if North Ferriby United made it. Hopefully we will be seeing John and Mark on 29th March. Before Ed left, Alan apologised for becoming agitated after the second Bath City goal, but Ed re-assured him that neither he nor Harry had heard him. I felt a little bit guilty for telling him off.

On our way back to the North West, we dissected the game. Alan is more positive than me and I know in his heart of hearts he thinks North Ferriby United are destined to lift the FA Trophy. Lady Luck has rarely been a friend of mine, so I tend to take the more pragmatic/cautious/negative view.

"It's a shame they didn't hold on to the win, but 2-2 is a good result for Ferriby. Bath won't enjoy going up there. That McCootie lad could have hit that shot 1000 times and it would only have gone in that once. Still, Ferriby are favourites now."

It seems an amazing thing to hear. North Ferriby United are favourites to get to Wembley. I thought back to the game refereed by Brad and Joel's schoolteacher, Michael Salisbury, when he gave a penalty to Boston United when they were already 1-0 up and as a consequence of the tackle, sent Danny Hone off. Ferriby would have been a million to one to reach Wembley then, now they were favourites. I thought about how disappointed we were when Ferriby equalised, just because we wanted to avoid a midweek trip to Boston. It wasn't because we didn't like North Ferriby United, it was just because of the thought of a long midweek trek to Boston the week before Christmas, even the Ferriby players didn't look overly delighted when Ryan Kendall equalised in the dying seconds. Now, half way through the Semi Final, we were grateful to Nicklin and Kendall for playing a huge role in bringing Ferriby so close to Wembley.

On our way home, we listened to the Manchester City v Newcastle United game on the radio, a 5-0 win putting Alan in even finer spirits. In what felt like no time, Alan was soon dropped at Crewe and I was back at our house. My Mum and Dad had called around to keep an eye on the children, as Alison had gone to work, so it was a relief to know my Mum was feeling better. I told my Dad about the soft penalty, but he was of the opinion that referees should have the courage to give more penalties for minor offences as a foul is a foul no matter where it takes place. It was hard to disagree.

Billy Heath, Ferriby's experienced manager, did not see things completely the same way as my Dad. I read on the internet that Heath felt that similar incidents had happened on several previous occasions during the game, at both ends and there was a lack of consistency from the ref. This was also a valid point. I am easily swayed.

I noticed John Rudkin was on Facebook so messaged him to see what he thought of the day, the penalty and whether the mood on the team coach home was one of positivity or despondency. John gave a very honest appraisal.

"I thought it was a penalty. The mood initially was we had thrown it away but as the beer set in, it was more positive, with things like we would have took the draw beforehand. We have nothing to fear and at our place, where we are very good, we can get the job done."

FINAL SCORE :- Bath City 2 North Ferriby United 2

Sunday 22nd February 2015

Buying the 'Non-League Paper' every Sunday morning is always a joy, but it becomes even more of a joy when North Ferriby United are heavily featured, as they have been today. Not that the front page was joyful. I didn't mind the main photo, Wrexham's Joe Clarke celebrating putting his team a goal up in their first leg win over Torquay United. The game finished 2-1 to Wrexham, denting my hopes of a Ferriby-Torquay United final.

It was the smaller picture on the front cover that was a painful reminder of yesterday, showing Bath City's Nick McCootie lining up to boot the ball into the back of the Ferriby net for his equalising goal. The photographs inside of the Bath-Ferriby game were no more positive for those with a Ferriby bias either, with a large one of Dave Pratt's penalty and another of Bath's McCootie and Stean celebrating the equaliser. Still, a whole page dedicated to a North Ferriby United game was great to see and reflected how far they had come in the competition. With a bit of luck, if Ferriby win next week, there will some photos of their players celebrating.

As we were directly behind the goal when Ferriby scored their two goals, our little band of eight have cropped up on several photos that were on the FA website, the North Ferriby United website and the local Hull papers. There is a cracker of Jason St Juste and Danny Clarke celebrating St Juste's goal, with a load of delighted Ferriby fans celebrating in the background, including the eight of us. Actually, six of us are celebrating, Ed and Harry are on the corner of the picture, looking a little disappointed. Ed is a great guy, but I hope next Saturday at quarter to five, he is equally disappointed when he hears the result from North Ferriby.

Tuesday 24th February 2015

North Ferriby United lost tonight 2-0 at home to Hednesford Town in a Conference North League game. It was no great surprise. With the vital Semi Final Second Leg taking place on Saturday, Billy Heath selected a starting eleven that bore no resemblance to the team that started against Bath City, with ten changes to the side. Only Adam Bolder started both games. If I was Bolder, I would be a bit worried that this hinted that I was going to be dropped for Saturday's game, either that or Heath has him down as a wiley old pro, who knows how to get through a game without too much impact on his ageing body.

I have been in touch with Jamie and he is intending on coming along on Saturday. There were only 265 fans in attendance when he last came to the 'Eon Visual Media Stadium', for the Hyde game, so I think he will get a bit of a shock at the weekend. John Rudkin thinks there will be around 1500 there, which in a tight little ground, should make for a brilliant atmosphere. I can't wait.

Saturday 28th February 2015 – FA Trophy Semi Final (Second Leg)

North Ferriby United v Bath City

Attendance – 1 871

Whatever happened, today was always going to be an emotional day. Having followed North Ferriby United to eight FA Trophy games this season, it would be heartbreaking to see them fall at the final pre-Wembley hurdle. I would be gutted for their players, their supporters and everyone associated with the club. From a selfish perspective, I would also be gutted for my book. I have written it in diary form and from a third of the way through North Ferriby United have taken it over. I knew should North Ferriby United lose, their supporters may still give it a go, but it would really only have a market for the diehard fan. Fans of Bath City and the winners of Wrexham and Torquay United may not be overly interested in how a small village side from near Hull managed to get from the Third Preliminary Round to the Semi Final.

One thing was for certain, this was going to be our fifth and final FA Trophy visit to North Ferriby United this season. Speaking to Alan during the week, he remained upbeat, Ferriby were going to win. I remained worried that Bath City turned a corner after an hour last week and they would not play as badly again. North Ferriby United players would either be telling their grandchildren about how they went to Wembley or they would be telling the tale of how they were leading 2-0 in the Semi Final first leg and then everything unravelled.

Unusually, Alan and I did not travel to the game together, nor did either of us go to Jamie's for a pre-game lunch. My eldest son, Brad was playing football this morning for Chorley District against Salford District in Sale, so I took him there, arranged for him to be given a lift home and left at half-time with them losing one-nil, which ended up as the Final Score. Brad played well (in goal) and is receiving some rave reviews from his coaches, which is great to hear.

I suggested to Alan that I could pick him up somewhere on the West side or North side of Manchester, but he said it was just as easy for him to get the train to North Ferriby and then he would jump in my car on the way home. Jamie is moving house soon to a new build in Beverley, so he arranged for his wife Amy to drop him back off at the ground on their way back from a morning trip to Beverley to check on its progress.

I didn't want to leave anything to chance so I was at the ground by one o'clock. Alan was even more cautious as he was there before me. As I arrived at the pathway that leads to the ground, alongside the allotments, so did the Bath City players, as they had just been let off their coach. I walked up the path right behind them and noticed there was no laughing and joking, they were almost silent. I took this to represent either a singleminded attitude and focus on the game or a sign of extreme nerves, perhaps it was both. I was going to joke with them that the little pathway wasn't exactly Wembley Way, but decided not to. Today, they felt like the opposition and being friendly and chatty with them, felt strangely unacceptable.

The Bath City players were ushered in through the gate, whilst I paid at the turnstile and bought my programme and raffle tickets to maintain my pre-match routine. There were already a lot of people milling around, two hours before kick off, a positive sign that there was going to be a bumper crowd. The first three people I saw were Alan Oliver, Chris Norrie and Chris Holbrough. The latter two were on edge, North Ferriby United means a huge amount to them and this was probably the biggest day in the club's history. I discovered Chris Holbrough is not only on the Management Committee, but also helps run the North Ferriby United Academy, taking in children from the age of four. If North Ferriby United were to reach Wembley, they would take a lot of the Junior sides down with them. There was no getting away from it, it was a massive day. Last year's Quarter Final defeat would be inconsequential relative to a loss in the Semi Final.

Alan had already been in the bar, which he said was already packed, but I wanted to say a quick hello to John Rudkin and Julie Martin. We had only met them a few times but John has always been so helpful in providing information for the book and raising our profile to the North Ferriby community, that he felt like a friend. John, as always, had his iPad with him, trying to manage an ever increasing number of Twitter followers and well wishers. He looked manically busy so I didn't want to bother him for too long, but thanked them both, shook John's hand and gave Julie a kiss and hoped the day ended perfectly for them.

Before I headed back out the bar, John introduced me to Nick Quantrill, a local crime fiction writer who has written three successful novels set in the Hull area with private investigator, Joe Geraghty as his central character. Nick is a keen supporter of Hull City and North Ferriby United, so we had a good chat about two topics close to my heart, football and writing.

Once outside, I spotted another writer, journalist Charlie Mullan from the Hull Daily Mail, who we had met at Bath. His article on mine and Alan's FA Trophy exploits had appeared in Thursday's paper, so Jamie had been instructed to go out and grab an extra couple of copies, which we intended to collect on the way home.

Charlie was another supporter who was excited but nervous as hell, as he knew what it meant to the club and the local community and was quick to admit that he had barely slept.

As Charlie went into the home dressing room, to do some pre-match interviews, I found Alan who was tucking into his pie and chips. Alan told me he had been having a chat with Ferriby's manager, Billy Heath.

"I asked him whether he was nervous," Alan said, "and he said he wasn't too bad and what will be, will be. I told him I could see it going to penalties and Billy said he didn't want that. I laughed and reminded him he had just said, 'what will be, will be'."

The wonderful thing about non-League football is that even on the biggest day in a club's history, everyone involved in the club, no matter how busy they are, will always spare you a few minutes. There are no massive egos at this level and the tight bond between everyone involved is obvious. If North Ferriby United did lose in the Semi Final, it would be disappointing not to have met John Colley, as he is highly thought of by everyone I speak to at the club and continues to bang my drum as loud as anyone, constantly telling people on social media about my writing. John was on Radio 2 yesterday, being interviewed about the game, but unfortunately due to work commitments wasn't going to be able to make it along. He said he was turning his office into a North Ferriby United shrine and had made sure he had the FA Trophy Final weekend booked off work in case the miracle happened and Ferriby made it.

As Alan finished his lunch, Jamie arrived, sporting a well maintained beard which earned me a ticking off from Alan for sporting an untidy one. My Mum doesn't give me as much grief about my beard as Alan. I told Al I had caught up with John and Julie in the bar and shook John's hand and gave Julie a kiss, as we may not see them again for a while if Ferriby lose.

"Snogging women in the clubhouse," Jamie jibed, "I bet that doesn't make it into the book. You're quite happy to write about Alan's exploits but you keep your own exploits under wraps, don't you?"

"I've missed you winding him up!" Alan laughed.

The stadium was filling up fast so we decided to go to the terrace at the far end of the ground, where we had stood for the first half of the game against Hyde. North Ferriby would, in all likelihood, be kicking in towards the goal by that terrace and it would be a good vantage point. With Alan being a foot smaller than Jamie and me, it would ensure he would have a good view of proceedings, as it is elevated slightly above pitch level. We chatted away merrily before kick off, as the crowd swelled to reach a fantastic 1 871. North Ferriby United taking ten supporters to Boston United, including Alan and me, now seemed like light years ago, as the whole area was now well aware of the team's achievements and were willing them on. I had brought my iPad with me to take a few pictures of the crowds, so a new round of ribbing began about how I was letting fame go to my head and how I used to take a disposable camera in the early days.

At five to three the players were out. Importantly, Adam Nicklin had recovered well enough from his ankle injury to be passed fit to play, although we were aware that he was not going to be 100% fit. Billy Heath had shuffled his pack, making a couple of changes to personnel and formation. Gregg Anderson came in to replace Mark Gray and Ryan Kendall replaced Adam Bolder, as Heath decided to go with a more aggressive 4-4-2 formation. The team selected for Tuesday night, with Bolder playing, was a clue after all.

The Bath City team looked far bigger than they had at Twerton Park. We didn't have a team sheet, just the programme, so at that point I didn't know if there were significant changes to the team or whether they had all been in the gym with Arnold Schwarzenegger for the week. I could spot two changes, Nick McCootie was rewarded for his wonder goal with a starting place and Ben Adelsbury's impressive cameo had also earned him a place in the eleven too. It transpired there was also a third change, with Dan Bowman coming off the bench, having failed to feature last week. The team probably weren't that much bigger, although McCootie is an imposing figure, they just looked bigger in a smaller, tighter stadium.

When the game kicked off, it was a role reversal from last week, with Bath City starting brightly. The game was only two minutes old when there was some neat interplay between the Bath forwards before Nick McCootie, closely guarded by Danny Hone, laid the ball out to the right wing to Sekani Simpson. Simpson put a high ball into the box, allowing McCootie time to drift to the back post, losing his marker and heading past Nicklin into the keeper's right hand bottom corner. Bath City were one up.

Like most of the home support, I had a sinking feeling. From two-nil up in the tie, North Ferriby United were now 3-2 down. At least North Ferriby United had eighty eight minutes to repair the damage, but I sensed that if Bath City went two up, they would learn lessons from Ferriby's mistakes from the first leg and make sure they closed the game out. The next goal was going to be vital.

North Ferriby United almost scored that next goal straight away. Sam Topliss pushed up along the right wing and sent a great ball over to the far post which was ideal for the towering Denton. He directed the ball back across the goal, but Jason Mellor, the Bath City keeper was equal to it and stretched out his left hand to push the ball wide.

The early goal had opened up proceedings and in a lively first half there were chances at both ends, but the clearer cut ones were falling to North Ferriby. In the 14th minute, Denton went down in the box, claiming he was pulled over by Phil Walsh. It appeared a valid claim but referee, David Webb disagreed. Ferriby's Captain Marvel, Liam King, was following up though and hit a powerful shot that was blocked by the opposition captain, Andy Gallinagh. When Ferriby managed to get beyond a committed Bath defence, they discovered Bath City keeper, Mellor, was in fine form. He made three smart saves from Ryan Kendall, who was looking his usual busy self, but when Ferriby finally managed to get past Mellor too, with a firm Denton header shortly before half-time, the ball bounced agonisingly off the post.

Throughout the first half, Bath City were looking dangerous on the break but after the early lapse, the North Ferriby defence was looking rock solid. Alan thought Bath City should have had a penalty after about half an hour, when Nicklin failed to gather a cross and clattered into Dan Ball. As a former goalkeeper, I thought it was more a coming together of two advancing players and thankfully the referee, Webb, agreed with me.

At half-time, the score remained one-nil to Bath City and they were only forty five minutes away from reaching Wembley for the first time in their 125 year history. I am sure Mark Stillman, their programme editor and all the rest of their large away contingent were feeling nervously excited, but I was feeling fed up. With Bath's keeper looking excellent and their defence looking resolute, it felt like Ferriby would have to conjure up something out of the ordinary to get back in the game.

At half time, Alan was telling us a story about getting the train across from Manchester with Dave Yeoman, a Ferriby fan from Warrington. Dave is a regular 'tweeter' and had spotted Al on the train and approached him, asking him if he was the groundhopper. Alan is enjoying being recognised and the admiration he is deservedly getting from fellow football fans for his football and charity exploits. It has certainly cranked up a level from last season.

What Alan did not enjoy, however, was the decision made by Jamie and me, at half time, to move towards the goal Ferriby would be attacking in the second half. The whole ground was crammed full and to be fair, when we decided to move, we didn't really give too much thought to the fact that Alan is a lot smaller than us. Jamie and I can normally see over the heads of most supporters, but as we moved around the ground, we realised there were very few vantage points that Alan would be able to see from, as most spots were three deep with supporters. As we headed past the goal that Bath City would be protecting in the second half, we passed Mark Gray, the Ferriby centre back, who had obviously been left out the squad altogether for this game. The fact he was tracksuited hinted that he was not injured. Gray is a good solid player, but his replacement at centre half, Gregg Anderson is equally dependable and with Matt Wilson and Danny Hone also accomplished centre backs, it must be a headscratcher for Billy Heath. He tends to put one centre back on the bench, but I remember thinking if North Ferriby United make it to Wembley, one of the four is likely to miss out altogether and with Wilson seemingly edging his way back into favour, Gray must have been feeling vulnerable. If Ferriby didn't score in the second half, it would be a problem they would never have.

As the players came out for the second half, we had still not found a place to stand that allowed Alan to see. He was starting to get grouchy. I could empathise, if I had a spectator who was nine inches taller than me, blocking my view, I would get pretty irritable too. Thankfully, that spectator would have to be seven feet tall for such a scenario to arise. A pair of stilettos or stilts are going to be on my shopping list for Al's next birthday, they may be a necessity in the latter stages of next season's FA Vase.

We ended up on the concrete embankment near the entrance, but as the half progressed, we edged further towards the players dressing rooms at half way, as it became harder and harder to see, even for Jamie and myself.

From what we could see through the masses, the second half had not started in as dramatic a fashion as the first half had been throughout. It was a bit stop start due to a number of injuries and ref David Webb began to get his book out, as the tackles were flying in. The first half chance fell to Tom Denton, about ten minutes in but he didn't get his usual power behind his header and the ball fell tamely to Mellor. Soon after, Ryan Kendall shot over the bar, but despite the majority of the game being played out in Bath City's half, Mellor was nowhere near as busy as he had been in the first half.

On the hour mark, we finally found a good vantage point near the halfway line. Chris Holbrough came to join us, as he thought Alan and I brought Ferriby good luck. He could have a point. Five minutes later, Liam King took a short throw in to Sam Topliss, deep into the Bath City half. Topliss sent a cross over that was headed clear, but Russell Fry picked up the loose ball, passed it to Liam King, who was still on the right wing and his cross was directed towards Denton on the far post. The ball was a little beyond Denton and as he leaned backwards, Bath City defender Phil Walsh had his arms around Denton's midriff and Denton fell to the floor, in a similar vein to the incident in the first half. This time, however, the referees decision was different, rather than wave play on, he pointed immediately to the spot.

It was another soft one. In my opinion, it was on a par with the penalty Bath City were awarded in the first leg and less of a penalty than the one in the first half. This season, Premier League players have taken it upon themselves to confront a referee en masse, when a decision goes against them, but like Ferriby in the first leg, Bath City took the decision like proper men. There were a few complaints but the players, on the whole, accepted the ref's decision. If only the multi-millionaires in the Premier League could behave in a similar manner.

Once again, like in the Quarter Final against Ebbsfleet United, it was down to Liam King to collect the ball and place it on the spot. In a half with very few chances this was a huge one. King had only ever taken the one previous penalty for North Ferriby and he was now handed the chance to convert the most important spot kick in Ferriby's history. I would have been petrified, King, a born leader with an apt surname, looked like calmness personified. King took a long run up, beginning from inside the 'D'. His approach and body language gave the impression he would be going to Mellor's left, but he foxed me and more importantly Mellor. As the keeper dived to his left, the ball was struck low and hard to his right and into the net. 1-1 and after having endured over an hour of a Bath City lead, the game and the tie were back to being all square.

Both sets of players had given it their all and for the last twenty five minutes, the game began to open up. With no longer having a lead to hold on to, Bath City began to push out and Nicklin became more involved but rarely had more than a tame effort to deal with. At the other end, Danny Clarke had a great chance to win it for Ferriby, but his effort was saved by Mellor before being cleared off the line by Gallinagh.

Having dominated most of the second half, in the dying minutes, Ferriby found themselves under extreme pressure and Bath City had two golden chances to win it. The first was created by the quick David Pratt, who played a ball to the unmarked Ben Adelsbury in the box. He had time to pick his spot and time passed in slow motion as he shot towards goal. I was expecting the net to ripple and for the Bath City players to wheel away in delight, but thankfully the ball drifted wide. Moments later, Bath were presented with another chance, but as Topliss closed him down, Andy Watkins snatched at his shot and it went over the bar. Soon after, the final whistle blew and the game was heading for extra time.

Everyone in the ground was nervous. A mistake now could haunt a player for the rest of his life. I was distracted from my own nerves by a cheerful little boy, about eighteen months old, who was being held up by his mother.

"Look, there's Daddy! Wave to Daddy!"

The mother, an attractive dark haired lady in her twenties was holding her son up and pointing towards the North Ferriby United squad who were receiving a touchline team talk from Billy Heath.

"Who's his Daddy?" I enquired of the lady.

"Matthew Wilson," she replied.

I immediately felt a sense of guilt. Most of the North Ferriby United squad had received some positive comments throughout my book, but the only mention of Wilson that I could recall was his karate chop tackle in the Mickleover Sports game. He was unlikely to have been mentioned again, as he had not featured in the FA Trophy since. The feedback from supporters was that he was a very good player but had discipline problems and was a walking yellow card. He was obviously a much loved father and family man though and I remember hoping that he would come on and either score from a corner or strike the winning penalty.

I have seen Everton in many FA Cup Semi Finals and Finals and have to admit to feeling just as nervous watching this game. It was on a knife edge and within an hour, there would be mass celebrations, recriminations and tears. As is always the case in sport, for every winner, there is a loser and no matter how equally matched these two teams were, the FA Trophy finalist was soon to be decided. News was coming through that Wrexham had eased past Torquay United 3-0, winning 5-1 on aggregate. It was impossible to guess who their opponent would be, but after everything we had been through with North Ferriby United, I don't think I could have wanted them to win more if I had supported them for forty years and owned an allotment in the field next door.

North Ferriby United are a fit side and started the first half of extra time in the ascendency. Four minutes in, Jason St Juste sped along the left and powered a cross along the six yard line. Denton stretched his long right leg out for it but didn't manage to get the solid contact needed to direct the ball into the net and his slight touch directed the ball wide. More than a thousand supporters held their head in their hands as though it was a massive game of Simon says.

There were no further golden chances in the first half of extra time, but thirteen minutes in, Russell Fry tripped Bath City's Andy Watkins and was given a second yellow card. If North Ferriby United were going to get to Wembley now, they would have to do it the hard way. Bath City were given seventeen minutes to capitalise on their numerical advantage.

"I'd settle for penalties now," I said to Alan and Jamie as soon as the red card was brandished.

Despite being a man short, in the second half of extra time, North Ferriby United didn't settle for penalties and in fact, went charging forward looking for the elusive winner. Gregg Anderson was up for a free kick two minutes into the second half of extra time and the centre half managed to temporarily fool Ferriby fans on the far side of the pitch into thinking he had scored, as his effort rippled the net, but unfortunately it was only the side netting. Anderson had been in and out the side this season, persistent shoulder problems playing a part and looked shattered, so was replaced for the final nine minutes by Matt Wilson. I thought he had been excellent and was definitely a crowd favourite as the loud applause he received testified.

Just before Anderson had departed his fellow centre half, Danny Hone, had saved the day. Bath City's Ross Stearn fired in a shot that looked like a goal from the moment it left his boot, beating Nicklin, but thankfully Hone was on the line to clear.

In the final ten minutes, there were half chances at either end but nothing came of any of them and after two hours of dramatic football, David Webb brought matters to a close. Who was going to Wembley and who was going to watch the final on BT Sport, would now be decided by penalties.

As both teams decided their penalty takers, I found something new to concern me. Adam Nicklin had thankfully not been called in to action too often, but when he had, he had looked troubled by his problem ankle. With Nicklin half-injured for North Ferriby and Mellor in inspired and confident form for Bath City, were the away team now the more likely to triumph? I feared North Ferriby United were about to fall out of the Trophy in the most agonising way possible.

Whilst I agonised, Jamie expressed his excitement. He had never witnessed the drama of penalties live before and was looking forward to seeing how it played out.

"Are you coming to the Final if Ferriby get there?" I asked.

"No, I'm off to see 'Show Me, Show Me' that day in Crewe."

"What the hell is 'Show Me, Show Me'?"

"It's a CBeebies programme, we are taking the little fella."

Jamie is such a proud father this didn't surprise me. I would have loved him to come to Wembley as he had been our most regular guest spectator, but understood his commitments to his young family. Anyway, Ferriby had to win first. Alan was confident, as always.

"Nicklin will be the hero, Cal, don't worry about that."

If he had been fully fit, I would have agreed. Having watched him move around tentatively for two hours, I was becoming more and more doubtful. I also had my doubts about the Ferriby penalty takers. Nathan Jarman was a regular penalty taker and he had come on to replace Ryan Kendall, so I was confident about his and was equally confident about Liam King's who had taken two great penalties so far in the competition, but after that, I was not sure who would be taking them. If Denton could take one with his head, that would be useful, but although he had good close control, I had never seen him strike a powerful shot. Unfortunately, whilst I was giving myself reasons to expect defeat, Ferriby lost the toss and the penalties were going to be taken at the end that was mainly filled with Bath City supporters. That was an extra reason. Could the final chapter of my book be the perfect Ferriby fairytale? We would soon see.

Bath City were to take the first penalty. David Pratt, who had thundered his penalty home in the first leg, was the first taker. Going first was always a psychological advantage, providing your first player scored. Like Bath City had done, I would always give the first penalty to the man most likely to score.

David Pratt ran up quickly as though he was again going to power home his shot, but just before he struck the ball, he tilted his ankle and placed a right footed shot low to Nicklin's left. It was not near enough to the corner though and Nicklin dived low and managed to get his body behind it and palm the ball away. My doubts about Nicklin's ability to save penalties with a dodgy ankle were already proved to be wrong. My mood changed immediately. I was now as confident as Alan Oliver, Ferriby were heading to Wembley!

My sense of optimism was heightened by the fact that Liam King was stepping up to take North Ferriby's first penalty. King had played a captain's role throughout and I was confident he would score. During extra time, when Tom Denton was flagging, King had given him a verbal earbashing for not tracking back. This 'King' would not order his troops forward from the rear, he would lead from the front. King began his now customary long run up and thumped his spot kick to Mellor's top right hand corner. Gordon Banks, Lev Yashin and Peter Schmeichel could all have been on the goal line at the same time and they wouldn't have stopped it. It was the perfect penalty. One penalty each gone. One-nil to North Ferriby United.

Next up for Bath City was Ross Stearn. He looked confident and struck the ball hard and low to Nicklin's right. Adam Nicklin has been a superstar throughout this competition and was not going to miss out on a Wembley appearance. It was a decent penalty, but once again Nicklin had anticipated which way it would go. He leapt low to his right and again palmed the ball away. The Romans of Bath City were in seriously trouble now and were almost certainly doomed if North Ferriby's next penalty went in. I was anxious to see who would take the responsibility. I breathed a sigh of relief when I saw it was Nathan Jarman. As a penalty taker, he would be used to the pressure.

Jarman ran up quickly but, like David Pratt, tilted his foot and attempted to place the ball into the keeper's left corner. Mellor was alive to the danger and leapt full stretch to his left, but it was better placed than Pratt's, finding its way into the bottom corner. Two penalties each gone and two-nil to North Ferriby United. The only way Bath City could win in five now was if they scored their next three and Ferriby missed their next three. The odds were stacked against it. The fat lady hadn't started singing yet, but she was gargling with TCP in anticipation.

With two of his team mates having already missed, there wasn't as much pressure on Bath's Ashley Kington, but he needed to score to keep the shoot out alive, which he did in convincing fashion, smashing the ball low to Nicklin's right. The keeper hardly moved. It was an excellent penalty. 2-1.

Third up for North Ferriby United was Adam Bolder. As an ex-professional with vast amounts of experience, I had been willing Billy Heath to bring him on for the penalties, which he duly did in the last minute of extra time. I couldn't believe I had forgotten about him in my pre-penalty panic. Bolder strode up as if it was all in a day's work and placed the ball low to Mellor's left. The keeper had anticipated it going to his right and had to look over his shoulder as the ball rolled in. 3-1 to North Ferriby United after three penalties. One more goal for North Ferriby United or one more miss by Bath City and that would be it.

With the minimum of fuss and the minimum of backlift, Frankie Artus scored Bath City's fourth penalty to make it 3-2, sending the ball low to Nicklin's right. It was now down to North Ferriby United's fourth penalty taker to be the hero of the hour. Who was it going to be? The answer was Jason St Juste.

Jason St Juste has been a key player in the North Ferriby United pursuit of the Trophy. In the first leg, he had created one goal and scored the other. He had torn Boston United apart away from home and was a handful against Ebbsfleet United. This was his moment. His time to be the hero.

Upon the referee's instruction, St Juste stood directly behind the ball, on the edge of the box, so it was difficult to guess which way he would be sending his penalty. Mellor may have noted that St Juste was a left footer and his natural instinct was to shoot across the body towards Mellor's left hand corner. As St Juste ran up, he leaned to his right and Mellor went left, but he lofted the ball to Mellor's right and into the back of the net. The miracle had happened, North Ferriby United had made it to Wembley.

Jason St Juste ran off to his right, arms outstretched, pretending to be an aeroplane. Adam Nicklin, despite his dodgy ankle, was the first to grab him, but seconds later he was mobbed by the whole team. A few seconds later, the whole squad were there and soon after that quite a few fans joined in too. It was a good natured pitch invasion though and no fans wanted to do anything other than pat the players on the back or give them a hug.

"That was fantastic," Jamie said, "I really enjoyed that. Who would have thought when you first came here, way back in November, that you would be following North Ferriby to Wembley, every step of the way. Unbelievable! Hang on, where's Alan?"

I was looking towards Jamie and away from the pitch, but did not have to turn around to know.

"He'll be on the pitch, mate!"

Sure enough, we both spotted Alan. He was there, shaking Billy Heath's hand, hugging Dave Yeoman, who had also ran on enthusiastically and patting several players on the back as they passed by. The celebrations on the pitch continued for some time and even I, Mr.Cautious, edged on to the pitch for a couple of minutes, when I spotted John Rudkin and Charlie Mullan celebrating.

I felt tremendously sorry for Bath City and their supporters, but this was a special day for a small village side and we enjoyed lapping up every second of the celebrations. My iPad was out and I took several pictures of Alan conducting affairs on the pitch and when he finally dragged himself off, we asked someone to take a picture of Jamie, Alan and me, with a load of celebratory fans in the background.

Of the twenty three rounds of football so far in the FA Cup and FA Trophy, this had been the highlight. There were many grown men and women in tears. The players know many of the regular fans and they collectively embraced. I don't know North Ferriby United's Chairman, Les Hare, but those that do, say he is a wonderful man. He has been Chairman for seventeen years and all the hard work must feel more than worth it on days like today. He looked proud and emotional. Reaching the Final is not going to boost the club's bank balance like an FA Cup run, but it will provide an unforgettable day at Wembley. The players will tell their children and their grandchildren about their Semi Final victory and their trip to Wembley. The icing on the cake now, would be if North Ferriby United went to Wembley and came back with the Trophy. The way this story has panned out so far, maybe it is written in the stars. It certainly does not feel beyond them. We certainly feel privileged to have been able to witness this incredible story taking place before our eyes.

Alan Oliver, a Manchester City fan, might not thank me for using this quote but as Sir Alex Ferguson once said, "Football, bloody hell!"

FINAL SCORE :- North Ferriby United 1 Bath City 1 (4-2 on penalties)

<u>Sunday 1st March 2015</u>

What a great way to start a Sunday! I went with Joel to help out on his paper round this morning and gave him £1.50 to get me 'The Non-League Paper'. When he brought it to me, it was a fantastic feeling to see a close up picture of North Ferriby United's captain Liam King on the front cover, arms aloft, hands clenched punching the air in delight, with a smile as wide as the Humber Bridge. The front page headline was "Villagers Party On" and the caption headline was 'King For A Day'.

According to the paper, North Ferriby United are only the fourth side to reach Wembley in both the FA Vase and now the FA Trophy, Hillingdon Borough, Tamworth and Forest Green being the other three. North Ferriby lost their Vase final in 1997 against Whitby, but something tells me they aren't going to be losing this one. I know Wrexham are a professional club and their wage bill must be massive relative to North Ferriby United's, their players should be fitter and their support will be bigger and more vocal, but this is a fairytale and fairytales are only supposed to have a happy ending.

Wednesday 4th March 2015

I bought our tickets for the FA Trophy Final today. The tickets are at a discount until tomorrow, at £20 each, instead of the usual £30, but there was a further discount down to a bargain £15, if you bought in a block of 15 or more. I checked to see if we could get to fifteen and we have just scraped home.

Working in tandem with John Colley, who I will finally get to meet at Wembley, I managed to get eight of us to go and John is bringing seven. Our eight are me, Alison, Alan Oliver, Phil Cooper (who came to the first game of the FA Trophy and is now coming to the last), Gordon Johnson (who came to Farnborough) and his son, Kieran and Mark and John Goodchild (who came to Bath City). It is still 25 days away but it is like a countdown to Christmas.

As well as John Colley, the other North Ferriby United fan I hope I get to meet at Wembley is a 19 year old lad called Sam Shepherd. He watches North Ferriby United, home and away, and writes a regular blog on their performances. In an age when a lot of lads his age won't give non-League football a second glance, Sam has been rewarded for his loyalty to his local team by getting to see them at Wembley. I am sure if Mickleover Sports had knocked Ferriby out in the Third Qualifying Round, Sam's loyalty would not have diminished but when you put the hard yards in, it is fantastic to be rewarded with such a special trip.

After the highs of Saturday, normality has already returned for Sam and the North Ferriby United players and officials. Tonight they travelled to Oxford City and played in front of 177 people, as they drew 1-1.

Tuesday 24th March 2015

I have deliberately not added to the entries in this book for three weeks. After the excitement of the Semi Final, I didn't want to bore readers with minor details prior to the Final. The game on Sunday will be massive and will hopefully be a good enough game to be written about in great detail, so I thought I would just update with the interesting aspects of the build up.

Importantly, it looks like Billy Heath will have a fully fit squad to choose from. The biggest doubt has been Adam Nicklin, who has not played since the Semi Final victory but he is now back in training and Billy Heath reports that he will be fit for Sunday. The players and officials are heading down to London on Friday and are apparently going to be guests of the Football Association on Friday night, at Wembley, as England entertain Lithuania in a European Championship Qualifier. Then, on Saturday morning, thanks to Hull City manager, Steve Bruce's friendship with Sam Allardyce, the West Ham United boss, the Ferriby players will train at West Ham United's training ground in Chadwell Heath.

With regards to my own plans for the weekend, Alison and I are stopping in the Holiday Inn in Hemel Hempstead on Saturday night. I will then drive over to Harrow on the Hill and get the tube to Wembley Park from there. A lot of Ferriby fans have arranged to meet up at 'The Torch' pub, just up the road from Wembley Park, so our fifteen have also agreed to meet there.

Typically, Alan is using the Wembley weekend to tick off another new ground. He is going to head to St Albans on the Saturday before staying the night in Watford and meeting Phil Cooper at Euston on Sunday morning.

Sunday 29th March 2015 – FA Trophy Final

North Ferriby United v Wrexham

Attendance – 14 585

It may seem strange to some people, but without a shadow of a doubt, I woke up this morning far more excited about the FA Trophy Final, than I had been for last year's FA Cup Final. One of the bookmakers advertising slogans currently is 'It Matters More When There's Money On It', but the truth is, it matters more when one of the teams matters to you. After this season's FA Trophy trail, North Ferriby United mean a lot to me. In an odd way, for the rest of my life, part of me will be a 'Villager' now.

Alison and I had a relaxing stopover in the Holiday Inn, just outside Hemel Hempstead. There was a swimming pool there, so yesterday afternoon whilst Alison went for a swim, I took the opportunity to catch up on my daily fix of North Ferriby United news. On Friday, before setting off to Wembley, the team coach with all the players and officials onboard, made a pre-arranged stop at the North Ferriby Primary School, so all the local children could wave them off. It was a great idea and as the players all embarked from the coach in their green Wembley tracksuits, the delight on the faces of the children was fantastic to see. They waved flags, cheered and gave the players high fives. The club have made sure the local community have been made part of the Wembley experience and hopefully some of those children will be asking their Mums and Dads in future weeks if they can go down to the ground to watch the team play.

The other You Tube clip I watched was a North Ferriby United introduction to the players. As they are part-timers, it was interesting to note what they do in their working life. Tom Denton is a plasterer, Gregg Anderson runs a gardening business, Mark Gray is a plumber, Danny Clarke runs three businesses, Danny Hone is a dryliner, Jason St Juste is a trainee gas engineer, Nathan Peat said he was a professional model, which is very doubtful, and several of the others are students, teachers or involved in sport, including Adam Nicklin who is a gym manager and his boss is North Ferriby United's Assistant Manager, Mark Carroll.

Interestingly, Mark Carroll has been friends with Billy Heath since they were ten years old and have always been a coaching team since they started in management. They are both the same age as me, 44 and the FA Trophy Final was their 700th managerial game together. It is also the 150th Anniversary of Wrexham Football Club so they had an even more significant landmark that they wished to celebrate with an FA Trophy victory. Wrexham have had an up and down season in the Conference, currently languishing in mid-table and their fans felt like they needed the Trophy win to make up for a relatively poor season.

This morning, Alison and I checked out the hotel whilst Australia were heading for a comfortable cricketing World Cup victory over New Zealand. I drove to Harrow and we had a breakfast in a Wetherspoons before getting the tube to Wembley Park. We had arranged to meet in 'The Torch' pub at about 11:15, but as I was anxious not to be late, given I had fifteen tickets with me, we ended up being far too early and were at Wembley by quarter past ten.

It was pouring down but thankfully Alison is not precious about getting wet so we had an hour to have a walk up Wembley Way, show her the Bobby Moore statue and have a stroll around. As we were heading along an almost deserted Wembley Way, more than three hours before kick off, the big screen on the outside of the stadium flashed up, FA TROPHY FINAL, Wrexham v North Ferriby United. It was really emotional seeing North Ferriby United's name in lights and I had to remind myself to get a grip, as before November I didn't even know where they were from. This club has had a big effect on me in a short space of time.

As we were walking along Wembley Way, the first person I spotted was Charlie Mullan, from the Hull Daily Mail, so we stopped to have a chat and I introduced him to Alison. This was the first time I had seen him since the Semi Final victory and he said he had had a better night's sleep this time around. The victory would be great but defeat would not be as heartbreaking as a loss in the Semi Final, as you still have a wonderful day to reflect upon.

A few North Ferriby United fans arrived, including passionate Ferriby fan, Dave Farrow and his friends, so Charlie suggested I join them for a photo behind their flag, which he subsequently posted onto Twitter. It was continuing to pour down and the wind was picking up, so I'm not expecting a phone call from Vogue on the back of it.

We were in 'The Torch' by just after eleven and a few of the regular North Ferriby United fans were already in, including Chris Norrie and Chris Holbrough. We greet each other like old friends now, having shared this wonderful FA Trophy experience. Gordon Johnson and his son, Kieran were also there. They had been down on Friday for the England v Lithuania game, which England had won 4-0 and had driven back home before returning to Wembley this morning. Safe to say they are proper football fans. They have no allegiance to North Ferriby United or

Wrexham, just a genuine love for the game. Kieran is only twenty one, but is rising quickly through the refereeing ranks. He comes across as a well mannered, mature, knowledgeable lad and mixed in well with everyone. Pretty soon our whole group of fifteen had arrived with the exception of John Colley's Mum, Lynne who was travelling up by train from Exeter to see her first ever North Ferriby United game. What a great place to start!

John Colley was everything I expected him to be, friendly, enthusiastic, interesting and passionate about North Ferriby United. He knew some of the players very well and said Danny Clarke is a particularly great bloke and when John sponsored a game once, he said it was a proud moment when he gave Danny the 'Man of the Match' award. He seems like the type of man who is always full of life, always has a sunny disposition and someone who brightens your day just by being around, I can understand why he does so well in his Sales role. As well as his Mum, he was with Nick Quantrill, the crime fiction writer (we have ordered his first book and look forward to reading it), Craig Mitchelson, John's wife, Helen, who like Alison had never previously been to Wembley, Helen's brother Kevin Ryan and his fiancée Claire McCummesty.

John and Mark Goodchild soon arrived too and Alison was really pleased to see them, as they had been great neighbours for three years. Then finally, Alan Oliver and Phil Cooper arrived last, as Phil's train had been delayed. Phil is a gentleman and it's always great to have a chat with him and Alan was on a high like I had never seen him before. I've never seen Alan drunk, but I imagine this was as close as an insight as I would ever get as to how he was under the influence, before he packed the drink in three years ago. He was loud, chatty, funny, excitable and on edge. When he saw a lady face painting Chris Norrie's face green and white, Alan was desperate to get in on the act, asking her if she would paint an Adam Ant like green stripe across his face.

Alan hates half and half scarves so we managed to find a young lady with a half and half North Ferriby United and Wrexham scarf, so asked her to hold it up in the background as we took photos of Al getting his face done. He wasn't happy when he saw them and jokingly had a few cursory words aimed at Gordon Johnson that would have made Michael Reid, Warrington Town's manager blush. Well, actually, I'm sure it wouldn't.

Alison had never met Alan before.

"Is he always this mad?" she asked.

"He's always mad, but not this mad!"

Once Alan's face was painted North Ferriby United green, we headed up to Wembley. Alison was hugely impressed when she entered the stadium, but less impressed when she saw where we were sitting. We were in the 22nd row back, but the strong wind was blowing our way and we were all set for a further soaking. Luckily, we had dressed accordingly, but there was no way on a day like today that a bit of rain would dampen our spirits.

We were all very interested in seeing the side Billy Heath had selected and also see who had made it on to the substitutes bench. Matt Wilson had found himself back in the side for all the recent games, so the competition for the centre back slots had become even more fierce than it had ever been. Danny Hone has probably been the stand out centre back for me, as he has that extra yard of pace, but it was impossible to guess who out of the other three centre backs would play alongside him, who would be on the bench and who would miss out altogether.

When the team came up on the scoreboards, I was a little surprised to see Matt Wilson selected, but even more surprised to see Gregg Anderson miss out altogether, as he had started in the Semi Final second leg. Mark Gray was on the bench. Anderson had bought tickets for around eighty of his friends and family, so it was a real shame that he had not made the squad, but Billy Heath was there to pick a side and a squad that he felt gave him the best chance of winning the Trophy, so he could not afford to allow sentimentality to play its part. Anderson must have been shattered by the news, but still warmed up with the lads prior to kick off and then changed into his suit and joined the North Ferriby United fans pitchside.

As for the rest of the team, Heath went with the 4-5-1 formation that he had used at Bath City, which meant Tom Denton was a sole forward and his striking partners Ryan Kendall and Nathan Jarman had to make do with a place on the bench. The side was :- Adam Nicklin, Sam Topliss, Josh Wilde, Danny Hone, Matt Wilson, Danny Clarke, Adam Bolder, Russell Fry, Liam King (captain), Jason St Juste, Tom Denton. Substitutes :- Tom Nicholson, Mark Gray, Nathan Jarman, Ryan Kendall and Nathan Peat.

Gregg Anderson was not the only player who had played a part in the FA Trophy campaign to totally miss out. Louis Bruce and Jonathan D'Laryea were a couple of others who sprang to mind who had not made the bench.

With regards to the Wrexham team, the one player who had the highest profile amongst the North Ferriby United contingent was Dean Keates. The 36 year old midfielder is only 5 feet 5 inches tall, but height is not a necessity when you have as much natural ability as Keates. He is fondly remembered by Ferriby fans as he had two years at Hull City, apparently scoring their first goal at the KC Stadium and during his spell at Hull, from 2002-2004, he lived in Brough, the next village along from North Ferriby. When the teams were read out over the tannoy system, Keates was the only Wrexham player given a cheer at our end.

Once the game kicked off, the first thing that struck me was that Adam Nicklin in the North Ferriby United goal was not totally over his ankle injury. He normally ground kicks confidently and can land a ball midway between half way and the opposition goal. Straight from the start his kicks were poor and were barely making the centre circle. Alan, always good for an interesting statistic, told me that Ferriby's ground was the same width as Wembley but five yards shorter from goal to goal, so it wasn't as though the pitch was far bigger. Nicklin wasn't moving around his area too comfortably either, he wasn't limping but his freedom of movement looked impaired. It seemed a risk to be playing him and it was a real shame as he is such an impressive keeper and I felt the spectators in the ground and the viewers on BT Sport were not getting to see him in his true light.

The first few minutes of the game were scrappy, but as the teams settled down, it was Wrexham who were playing the neater football, especially down their left side. After only ten minutes, Connor Jennings slipped a ball through to Joe Clarke who darted along the left wing past Topliss. Clarke looked up and cut a ball back from the byline. Matt Wilson desperately tried to clear the danger, but the precision of the pass caught him off balance and Louis Moult struck a low left footed shot across the body of Nicklin, who managed to get a hand to it but the ball still crept into the left corner of the keeper's net. 1-0 to Wrexham.

Wrexham were looking like a young, vibrant, footballing side but the experience of Dean Keates was also important as he was central to a lot of what they did. The Ferriby defence was looking solid though and Wrexham were restricted to a few half chances. At the other end, Danny Clarke, who had been Ferriby's most impressive player of the half, had a shot saved by Wrexham keeper Coughlin and referee Michael Oliver waved away a handball shout from Jason St Juste after a cross struck a Wrexham defender. In spells, Jason St Juste was also looking dangerous and it appeared that if North Ferriby United were to get back in the game, it would come from an opportunity fashioned by one of their midfield wide men. At half time the score remained 1-0, which was a fair reflection of the play as Wrexham were the better team without creating too many chances for Moult, who looked dangerous every time he received the ball.

At half time, Alison wanted to get a coffee to warm herself up, so I accompanied her, but began to get twitchy once it got to half past two and we still hadn't been served. We just managed to get to the entrance to our block as the second half got underway, but stayed there to watch an early free kick from Wrexham come to nothing.

At one-nil, it would only take one moment of magic to turn the game but a second goal for Wrexham could turn the game into a procession. Six minutes in, Connor Jennings had a great opportunity to score a second but after beating Nicklin, Danny Hone managed to clear the ball off the line. A few minutes later, Wrexham did get their second. After some neat play on the left involving Keates, the ball was played to Jennings, who cut inside, played a one-two and then released Jay Harris, who had made an intelligent run to Jennings right. The switch of play had caught out the two Ferriby centre halves, who had drifted to their right, causing Josh Wilde to fill in centrally and leaving acres of space for Harris to exploit. Once Jennings found him with an inch perfect pass, he had time and space to push the ball in front of him with his first touch and then coolly beat Nicklin at his near post with his second. 2-0 to Wrexham!

On several occasions during their FA Trophy run, North Ferriby United had bounced back from adversity, but I couldn't see a way back this time. Wrexham were a professional club, were technically better and would prove to be fitter as the game progressed. I just hoped that Ferriby would continue to make a game of it and if possible, score a goal to give their fans a moment to cheer and the player who scored it a moment to treasure.

After the second goal, filled with confidence, Wrexham began to dominate. Billy Heath had to go looking for a goal so brought Nathan Jarman on for Adam Bolder and went to 4-4-2 but Bolder's absence naturally created more gaps in midfield. Tom Denton was having to come back to defend set pieces and his aerial presence was being seen much more defensively than offensively. Both Danny Clarke and Jason St Juste were however, continuing to have excellent games and each time Ferriby broke forward, they did look threatening. Ferriby's first really good chance of the game came after 72 minutes when Danny Hone headed over from a St Juste corner.

After this chance, I received a text from Sean O'Donnell, my old University mate from Omagh, County Tyrone. He had been following our FA Trophy journey with interest. His text simply said,

"End of the dream for North Ferriby…on BT Sports now…Wrexham are a class above."

Perhaps it was wrong for anyone to expect any more from North Ferriby. They had given their all, had done remarkably well to reach the Final and had battled admirably against a professional side. A 2-0 defeat was no shame. I had already decided to put 'Ferriby Fairytale' into the title of my book and the whole weekend was a fairytale, no matter what the final scoreline was.

"Have you enjoyed your day, Alison?" a cheerful John Colley asked.

"Yes, it's been brilliant," Alison replied, "it's just a shame about the result."

"It's not over yet," John replied, "there's still time."

I admired John's optimism, but thought it was totally unfounded. There were around fifteen minutes left for Ferriby to score two goals, in the previous 75 minutes, their opportunities to score one had been infrequent.

"I'm blaming, Alison and Phil," I joked, "Alan and I have never seen Ferriby lose and we bring this pair along and it all unravels."

"I thought I'd get the blame," Alison replied.

I should have know better than to write North Ferriby United off. Within a couple of minutes, Denton played a nice ball through to Jarman and with Denton having had to drop deep to collect the ball, Jarman was isolated. To give him an option, Danny Clarke sprinted forward. Clarke's ability to run and run puts Forrest Gump to shame and Jarman attempted to find him with a delicately weighted, flighted pass into the box. One of the Wrexham centre backs attempted to cut the ball out, but only managed to prod it halfway between Clarke and the Wrexham keeper, Coughlin. Both sprinted towards it, but Clarke had the additional pace required and pushed the ball past the keeper with his left foot before being clattered.

It was a clear penalty and Michael Oliver pointed to the spot. It could be argued that Coughlin, as last man, could have seen red, but Oliver decided a yellow would suffice.

Liam King had already scored three penalties in the FA Trophy campaign and now, if North Ferriby United were to be given even a glimmer of hope, King had to score his fourth. It was asking a lot, but King took his now traditional long run up and lifted the ball high to Coughlin's right. The keeper guessed right but it was so firmly struck that he had no chance. It was a carbon copy of the penalty he had taken in the shoot out against Bath City. 2-1 and North Ferriby United had a lifeline.

At this point, it is worth pointing out that the goal came from North Ferriby's 'never say die' attitude. Faced with a mammoth task, some side's heads may have gone down, but until the final whistle blows that never happens at North Ferriby. Clarke set off on his blistering run to support his team mate and his spirit and determination had paid dividends.

There were still around fourteen minutes left and the North Ferriby United players and fans were now full of belief. Billy Heath decided this was not going to be a day he would reflect upon and die wondering, so made a further attacking substitution replacing Russell Fry with Ryan Kendall and switching to a 4-3-3 formation. With St Juste and Clarke pushing on, it was near enough 4-1-5 and Liam King isn't exactly a defensive midfielder either.

Ryan Kendall always struck me as a man who would relish a big occasion. Whenever there are any clips from goal celebrations or dressing room antics, posted by John Rudkin on to Twitter or Facebook, Kendall is always in the thick of the action. He seems to thrive on being centre stage. As he ran on the pitch, he did a little shimmy. He was only possibly getting ten minutes to make a difference, but hell, he was going to enjoy every second.

In our row, we were growing increasingly excited by the prospect of an equaliser. Alan felt it was going to happen, John Goodchild was less sure.

"If North Ferriby make it 2-2, Alan, I will kiss your baldy head," John joked.

Jason St Juste had worked tirelessly up the left wing and his speed and trickery had created all sorts of problems. In the 85th minute when a heavily weighted ball was played out to the left, it looked for all the world that it would roll off harmlessly for a Wrexham throw in. St Juste had other ideas. Manny Smith, the Wrexham defender tracked across, not really anticipating that St Juste would keep it in, but once he did, Smith was there as cover. St Juste cut inside, attempted to dazzle Smith with a 'Ronaldoesque' stepover and then pushed the ball towards the byline before cutting it back through the legs of the helpless defender.

Ryan Kendall does not score goals for fun by lacking in intelligence. As St Juste set off on his run, Kendall sensed an opportunity and headed for the front post whilst Denton dropped to the back. As St Juste hit the byline, Kendall motioned as if he was going to get goal side of his marker, but then doubled back, just as St Juste crossed. Kendall prodded the ball, from six yards out, into the far corner of Coughlin's net. North Ferriby United had looked dead and buried, but amazingly it was now 2-2. The fans went wild and as I looked to my left, John Goodchild was grabbing Alan Oliver's head with two hands and planting a kiss on the top of it. What a game!

If there was going to be a winner in normal time, it was going to be North Ferriby United. Wrexham's players and fans looked stunned whilst the Ferriby players and fans were on cloud nine. The excited supporters roared their team on, every time they surged forward. In the 89th minute, John Colley was delighted to see Nathan Peat being brought on to replace Josh Wilde at left back. Peat is another much loved character at the club and at 32, is one of the elder statesmen. As he heads towards the twilight of his footballing career, a taste of Wembley is definitely something to savour. I am sure like the rest of his team, he wanted to seize the opportunity to leave with a winners medal.

In injury time, North Ferriby United had two excellent chances to win the game. Kendall tried to backheel a ball from just behind him into an empty net, but just failed to get the right connection and the ball struck a defender. Then, Danny Clarke hit a rasping shot that was excellently saved by Coughlin. Soon after, Michael Oliver blew his whistle to signal the end of the ninety minutes and send the game into extra time.

"It's a pity, from a North Ferriby perspective, that the whistle had to go," John Colley commented, "I just hope the momentum doesn't shift now Wrexham have time to compose themselves."

When extra time started, it soon became clear the momentum was not shifting. Dean Keates, who had played a part in everything positive Wrexham had been doing, had been replaced with the score at 2-1 and his calm composure was missed as North Ferriby United went for the jugular. There was a need for some caution though and Billy Heath reverted to 4-4-2 with Nathan Jarman going into a right midfield position with Danny Clarke playing more centrally.

Ten minutes into the first half of extra time, the ball was played to Jarman on the right side, inside his own half. Jarman thumped a cross field ball to St Juste who found himself in space and surged forwards, as he had many times previously. Kendall and Denton have a good understanding and once again Kendall provided the front post option and Denton the back. St Juste fired across a looping ball that was probably aimed for the huge Denton, but either the wind or a slight deflection took the sting out of the ball and rather than travelling to the far post it dropped to the near post. Kendall jumped high and managed to hang in the air long enough to out jump Harris by about a foot and nod the ball into the far corner of the net. 3-2 to North Ferriby United and around us bedlam broke out. This was absolutely sensational.

Jason St Juste is nicknamed Sanka after the 'Cool Runnings' character, so Kendall ran to the touchline and sat himself down to begin what has now become a traditional bobsleigh celebration. Six of his team mates joined in, including Tom Denton, who would probably hit his head on every tunnel if he sat in a real bobsleigh. After the celebrations, North Ferriby United had twenty minutes to hold on, for a dramatic victory and probably the greatest comeback the new Wembley had yet to witness.

Half-time in extra time was reached without further drama and when the second half began, we counted down every passing minute. Alan cursed the fact that there was a scoreboard clock, as everyone around us kept casting their eyes on it, begging it to go quicker. A lot of the Ferriby players were on their last legs after an energy sapping two hours of play, especially St Juste who had surged forward time after time. This did not stop Ferriby throwing bodies at every Wrexham half chance, but as time passed, Ferriby were forced deeper and deeper.

With two minutes left, Ferriby cleared a ball and it fell to Nathan Jarman, only ten yards outside his own box, but when he looked up, he realised he was the furthest Ferriby player forward. He surged forwards but Wrexham's Wes York sprinted after him and tackled from the side taking some of the ball and some of Jarman, leaving the Ferriby player sprawled on the floor. Michael Oliver had a good view of it and decided to wave play on, despite Jarman's protests. The ball was played along the Wrexham right before Connor Jennings sent a high ball into the box. The ball was partially cleared but fell to Louis Moult, fifteen yards out, who smashed the ball on the half volley past Nicklin and into the roof of the Ferriby net. It was a wonderful finish from perhaps Wrexham's best player on the day and agonisingly it was now 3-3. Seconds later, it was all over and for the second round in succession, North Ferriby United had penalties. Everyone in the North Ferriby United end gave their players a standing ovation. The fourteen players had all played their part and they had provided an unforgettable final in tough conditions.

As both sides gathered together to pick their penalty takers, I felt supremely confident. Wrexham had beaten Grimsby Town to lift the Trophy in 2013 and had won twice this season on penalties, but North Ferriby United had an even more recent experience of winning a penalty shootout. Adam Nicklin may not be fully fit, but he still knew how to stop a penalty, as he had showed in the Semi Final. Only two things bothered me. Firstly, Adam Bolder, one of the penalty scorers in the Semi Final shootout had been substituted, so they could not call upon his vast experience and secondly, Jason St Juste, who had been named 'Man Of The Match' looked absolutely spent. Could they rely on him to score again? I had my doubts. I reminded myself I was wrong more often than I was right with these premonitions.

After ten fantastic rounds of FA Trophy football and after nine games of following North Ferriby United, their place in history would be decided by spot kicks. I took it as a positive that in a similar manner to the Semi Final, Liam King lost the toss. North Ferriby United would take the first penalty but they would be taken at the end of the Wrexham supporters. North Ferriby United players are not fazed by adversity and I knew this would not bother them a jot.

First up was Liam King. This was the Ferriby captain's fifth penalty of the FA Trophy campaign. I would have put my mortgage on him scoring. King took his usual run up and for the third consecutive time hit the ball in the exact same spot, high to the goalkeeper's right. Coughlin had anticipated that King would change sides and go to his left, but he had been mentally outfoxed by the 'Village King'. 1-0.

Wrexham's first penalty taker was Wes York. He seemed calm and collected and proved to be, steering the ball to Nicklin's left as the keeper guessed it was heading right. 1-1.

Second up for North Ferriby United was Nathan Jarman, a regular penalty taker. With no messing about, Jarman put the ball exactly where York had just put it and like Nicklin, Coughlin went the wrong way. 2-1.

Wrexham's next spot kick was to be taken by Andy Bishop. The turnaround from one penalty taker to the next seemed particularly quick as no-one wanted to deliberate and allow the pressure of the occasion to get to them. Bishop smashed the ball into Nicklin's right corner. The keeper hardly moved. 2-2.

Ryan Kendall was up third for Ferriby. He wasn't on the field for the Semi Final penalties, having been replaced by Nathan Jarman, but he was already having a brilliant day, scoring two goals, so I knew his confidence would be sky high. Kendall strode up confidently, but got under the ball a little too much. His lofted strike to Coughlin's left, hit the underside of the bar, bounced then span out. The Wrexham fans and goalkeeper began to celebrate but the question was, where had the ball bounced? Michael Oliver checked with his Assistant Referee, ascertained it had bounced beyond the goal line and quickly gave a goal. TV cameras revealed it was the correct decision. Kendall cheekily cupped his ear to the Wrexham fans, then wiped the sweat from his brow. Despite only being on the field of play since the 80th minute, he had scored a Wembley hat-trick of sorts. 3-2 to North Ferriby United.

Third up for Wrexham was Connor Jennings, who I felt had had an excellent game. He went low and to Adam Nicklin's left, but Nicklin anticipated it correctly, dragging the ball in to his grateful body. Still 3-2 and advantage North Ferriby United after three penalties each.

This was the moment that North Ferriby United needed Adam Bolder or perhaps a change in the law that would allow Liam King to take another. Instead, they had a weary Jason St Juste. "Sanka" had scored the winning penalty in the Semi Final, could he put Ferriby within an inch of an historic Trophy victory? St Juste went to Coughlin's right, but he didn't get enough elevation and it was at a level that is often described as 'a good height for a goalkeeper'. Coughlin gratefully parried clear. One penalty missed each, but Wrexham still needed to score their fourth penalty to level.

Neil Ashton was Wrexham's fourth penalty taker. Ashton is apparently a regular spot kick taker for the Welsh club, but his penalty was very similar to Jason

St Juste's, the ball flew at chest level to Nicklin's right. The keeper, like Coughlin before him, guessed correctly and pushed the ball to safety.

As the score was now 3-2 after four penalties each, it meant that if North Ferriby United scored their fifth penalty, the FA Trophy was theirs. The massive figure of Tom Denton strode forward from the halfway line.

As Denton was walking up, John Colley turned towards me. He was already aware of the title of my book.

"Look Calvin," he said, "it's Tom Denton, the 'Brutal Giant' of your title. What a perfect, fairytale ending if Denton scores this."

Denton looked hesitant, but the way he moves, he always looks hesitant, perhaps he is just laid back. Denton ran up, picked his spot and struck the ball low to Coughlin's left. It was an accurate penalty but lacked power and gave Coughlin a chance. The keeper was down quickly and his outstretched left hand scooped the ball off the goal line and away. It wasn't the greatest ever penalty but Denton was a little unlucky as it was a great save. Still 3-2 with one penalty left.

When I saw Wrexham's final penalty taker was Louis Moult, my heart sank. Some people you just know from their body language are very unlikely to miss. Moult had been fantastic during the game and as he walked up to the ball, I did not think for a single second that he would miss. In a supremely confident manner, Moult smashed the ball low into Nicklin's right hand corner. Like Kendall, Moult had also completed a hat-trick of sorts. 3-3 and now it was sudden death.

Matt Wilson was North Ferriby United's sixth penalty taker. Wilson had had a strong game, more than justifying his starting position. I felt he had to make his penalty his most memorable moment of his FA Trophy, because as things stood, my mind kept harping back to his flying tackle against Mickleover Sports. If this went in, I would attempt to delete that memory. This was a moment that he could tell his little boy about when he was older.

Wilson ran up and hammered the ball hard and straight. Coughlin guessed left. 4-3 to North Ferriby United. Well done Matt Wilson!

Blaine Hudson was up next for Wrexham. If he missed, North Ferriby United were winners, but Hudson replicated Wilson's penalty, hitting it hard and straight, a good option in the circumstances. 4-4!

Nathan Peat was next. North Ferriby United's seventh penalty taker. As John Colley had mentioned how good a bloke he was, I particularly didn't want him to be etched in North Ferriby United's history as the man who missed the penalty that lost the club the Trophy. The fact that he was left footed comforted me. Left footers are harder for goalkeepers to second guess. Peat absolutely smashed his penalty. It was high and to Coughlin's right. The keeper was nowhere near it, but if he had been, he would have probably been carried into the net and through the net with it. If you are old enough to remember 'Hot Shot Hamish', that's the sort of penalty it was. Unstoppable. 5-4 to North Ferriby United.

Steve Tomassen was up next for Wrexham. He had probably been hoping his turn would never come, but now it was here. After several successive predecessors had opted for power, Tomassen opted to go for accuracy. He sent his spot kick low to Adam Nicklin's left. Nicklin guessed right and landed on top of the ball, before gathering it in to his body. NORTH FERRIBY UNITED HAD WON!

Adam Nicklin once again was North Ferriby United's hero. He ran away jubilantly, evading his team mates and sprinting towards the North Ferriby United fans down the other end of the pitch. He shared a quick hug with fellow keeper Tom Nicholson, but significantly the first outfield player to catch him was captain, Liam King. King had scored five penalties during the FA Trophy campaign, in total, Adam Nicklin had saved six. The first one, against Boston United, had kept them in the FA Trophy. The last one had won North Ferriby United the FA Trophy! How good did that sound!

Liam King and his fellow players would now climb the steps to the Royal Box and collect the Trophy. He was no longer just the 'Village King', he was the 'King of Wembley'.

In 'Another Saturday & Sweet FA', I had written that I did not believe the saying "Good Things Happen To Good People". As I watched the players, officials and supporters of North Ferriby United celebrate their FA Trophy victory, I knew on this occasion, I had been proved wrong.

FINAL SCORE :- North Ferriby United 3 Wrexham 3 (5-4 on penalties).

2015 FA TROPHY WINNERS – NORTH FERRIBY UNITED